JOHN BUNYAN

JOHN BUNYAN

From the pencil drawing by Robert White in the British Museum

JOHN BUNYAN

Maker of Myths

by

JACK LINDSAY

With 2 Illustrations

KENNIKAT PRESS
Port Washington, N. Y./London

TO

MARGARET SHAW

WITH THANKS FOR HELP

JOHN BUNYAN

First published 1937
Reissued in 1969 by Kennikat Press
Library of Congress Catalog Card No: 73-86039
SBN 8046-0623-4

Manufactured by Taylor Publishing Company   Dallas, Texas

FOREWORD

THIS book is a biography of Bunyan. But there would be no excuse for re-telling the story of Bunyan's life unless one were considering it from a new angle, with a new focus. The new focus is here provided by the attempt to relate Bunyan's work in particular, and the protestant movement in general, to the social forces from which they sprang. At the same time I have tried to analyse the myth-making faculty in Bunyan and to show how his allegories take their place in the world of symbolism and myth.

Although I have dealt in some detail with the important moments of Bunyan's life, it is with his four imaginative works that my chief business lay : *Grace Abounding, The Pilgrim's Progress, Mr. Badman* and *The Holy War*. I have scarcely touched on his other fifty odd works except in so far as they light up problems of his life or of his four main writings.

I mention in the text that a careful consideration of Bunyan's autobiographical writings convinced me that he was not only scrupulously telling the truth, but was also a man capable of telling it. I shall therefore deal here with the two objections that have been raised against *Grace Abounding*. He mentions how devoted he was (in the early days of the Commonwealth) to the parish priest, his high place, vestment, service ; so full of reverence for such priests ' supposing them ministers of God ', that he would have lain under their feet.

Also he tells how this parish priest once gave a sermon on the evil of breaking the Sabbath with ' labour, sports, or otherwise ' ; but he (Bunyan) went on with his games.

It is argued that under the Puritan Commonwealth such things as surplices and sunday-sports were impossible ; and that therefore Bunyan has at least got the sequence of his story mixed up. As the whole validity of *Grace Abounding* depends on the sequence and inter-relation of moods and ideas, this objection has to be met.

The facts are that there never was under the Commonwealth the kind of Puritan rule that is commonly imagined. The shattering of the Presbyterian edifice by the Independents made way for all sorts of diverse opinions and activities ; and though the extreme Puritans may have ruled all observances in one locality, there was laxity in another. The following quotations from the *Journal* of George Fox the Quaker will make this clear :

I was to bring people off from Jewish ceremonies . . . and from all their images and crosses, and sprinkling of infants, with all their holy days (so called) and all their vain traditions. (1649.)

About this time I was sorely exercised in . . . testifying against their wakes or feasts, may-games, sports, plays, and shows, which trained people up to vanity and looseness, and led them from the fear of God ; and the days

FOREWORD

they had set forth for holy-days were usually the time they most dishonoured God by these things. (1649.)

This much confirmed Judge Fell in the persuasion he had, that the priests were wrong; for he had thought formerly, as the generality of people then did, that they were sent from God. (1652.)

And in the old Parliament's day many people . . . left off their curious apparel and ribands and lace, and their sporting and feasting with priests and professors, and would not go to wakes or plays or shows. . . . Then the priests and professors raged exceedingly against us. . . . (1657.)

These passages imply that Fox and his group of protestors were very much in the minority; and they strongly support the details given by Bunyan of his state of mind about 1650.

JACK LINDSAY

June 1937

The drawing of Bunyan reproduced is that pencil-drawn on vellum by Robert White about 1679. The photo of John Bunyan, greengrocer of Portland Town, London, N.W., I owe to Mrs. Philip Coutts-Trotter; this Bunyan claimed to be a descendant of the great Bunyan, and there certainly seems a family-likeness. I include it here because it has just the right atmosphere for the Bunyan family. This greengrocer's shop, with the sturdy figure of J. Bunyan, admirably represents the world of which, and for which, Bunyan wrote.

A note on Sources will be found at the end of the book.

CONTENTS

JOHN BUNYAN

ILLUSTRATIONS

JOHN BUNYAN

Early Years

NEAR the hamlet of Harrowden a small cottage stood at the foot of a slight hill, between two streams. The spire of St. John's Church in Bedford could be seen from the top of a green hillock to the south. In this cottage, late in November 1628, John Bunyan was born. On the 30th he was baptised in the parish church of Elstow, a mile to the west of Harrowden. Thomas Bunyan, John's father, was a brazier or tinker. Thomas Bunyan, John's grandfather, was alive ; a petty chapman he called himself in his will. The Bunyans had long been settled in the neighbourhood, and once they had had a much higher status. Now there was nothing left them but that small house.

Their line went back to some feudal tenants of the Norman lords of a castle near Pulloxhill. The lordship changed hands, but the Bunyans kept their place. In 1199 one of them held land at Wilstead, about a mile from Elstow ; in 1327 we find a Bunyan living on the very spot where our John was born. In 1542, at the time of the dissolution of the Elstow abbey-lands, a Bunyan is named as a tenant of the manor.

From that point we see the Bunyans going downhill. Doubtless they were one of the many yeoman families whom the great capitalist wave, given momentum by the seizure of Church lands, engulfed. In 1548 a Thomas Bunyan sold three roods of land held at Harrowden. He set up a roadside inn on the way to Medbury. His wife took an important part in the business ; for she was continually presented at the manorial court for breaking the assize. Eleven times she was fined for overcharging ; seven times she paid a fine of a penny, and four times a fine of twopence. In 1547 Thomas himself was fined a penny. There is nothing unusual in this apparent equal division of responsibility between man and wife. Women took a large part in the life and work in the lower classes ; we find them in the records employed at jobs such as brewing, tempering mortar, drawing straw for thatch, and so on. And very strong-minded and vigorous they usually appear. The notion of woman as a closed-in domestic slave, as we know it in the final, Victorian phase, was by no means the rule. Man was considered as patriarchally superior to woman ; but in actual daily life among the working-classes there was something of an effective equality between the sexes, or at least a chance of give-and-take.

John Bunyan could not have known as much about his ancestors as we do ; for he had no means, even if he had had the wish, to search through old records. He most probably had never heard that one Ralph Buingnon, a priest, had murdered in 1219 another priest whose body was found at Totternhoe : for which act Ralph was hanged. But there must have been some tradition in the family of their fall from the status of securely landed yeomen to that of chapmen and tinkers. Even the inn on the coach-road was lost to them. The Bunyans were still living in the locality where their ancestors had owned land ; and the memory of their yeoman days must have persisted.

This fall in status, this loss of ownership in the productive sources of wealth, must be fixed in mind ; for from it derive certain basic emotions in Bunyan.

That he was acutely conscious of his social status is proved by his works. He describes his family as belonging to ' a low and inconsiderable generation . . . that rank which is meanest and most despised of all the families in the land '. This is an exaggeration. The Bunyans had not sunk to the very lowest strata of dispossessed vagabonds and hired workers ; they yet had the Harrowden cottage and a few personal belongings. Still, they were on the edge of abject poverty ; and the fact that Bunyan does feel the need to state the family position in such extreme terms is itself significant of his sensitiveness on the subject. The Bunyans were far closer to the hired-worker level than to that of the yeoman or tenant farmer.

One J. G., in a preface to Bunyan's *A Few Sighs*, defends the author's mean social position and the smallness of his learning by a reminder that Jesus also came from a humble trade ; and Bunyan ends his own preface to the book : ' I am thine, if thou wilt not be ashamed to own me, because of my low and contemptible descent in the world '. It is of

3

interest, as showing the part played in his mind by
this question of status, that in a later edition he
changed this sentence to, ' I am thine to serve in
the Lord Jesus '. When he made this change, he
was a successful man, acclaimed ; he no longer felt
the need to protest so much. But at the time of
A Few Sighs (1658) he was deeply concerned with his
social position. He says bitterly that some men
despise the Lazaruses of the Lord because they are not
gentlemen, because they cannot with Pontius Pilate
speak Hebrew, Greek, and Latin. And in the second
part of *The Pilgrim's Progress*, when quoting a tag of
Latin, *Ex Carne et Sanguine Christi*, he ponderously
adds a note to say, ' The Latin I borrow '.

The question of education was one about which
he was especially touchy. In a preface to Bunyan's
first book, the Bedford pastor John Burton, reflect-
ing Bunyan's own mood, declares :

This man is not chosen out of an earthly but out of the
heavenly university, the Church of Christ. . . . He hath
through grace taken those three heavenly degrees, to wit,
union with Christ, the anointing of the spirit, and experiences of the temptation of Satan, which do more fit
a man for that mighty work of preaching the Gospel than
all university learning and degrees that can be had.

In *Grace Abounding* Bunyan says that he had no
education except ' to the rate of other poor men's
children '. And what little he did learn he forgot
almost utterly. Elsewhere he says, ' I never went to
school to Aristotle and Plato, but was brought up at
my father's house in a very mean condition, among a
company of poor countrymen '. Even near the end

of his life when a well-known author and preacher, he was (declares a friend) ' misrepresented upon the account of his education '.

Perhaps he went to some village school at Elstow or Harrowden, where some old woman or decayed church reader gave a few elementary lessons. Perhaps he walked along the bridle-road, by the line of willow-trees, met the main road at the leper-house and went into Bedford to the Free School. But that would have meant some four miles walk daily. And the Free School does not seem to have been efficiently run. About the time when Bunyan was nine or ten years old, the schoolmaster was accused of grossly neglecting his duties, treating his pupils cruelly, and spending his time in night-walking and tavern-drinking.

We may take Bunyan's word that he learned nothing except the rudiments of reading and writing. He was to all intents and purposes a mere illiterate peasant before ' grace ' stirred in his soul. We may call him proletarian in the sense that he is a working-man who writes out of his class experience. But we must deny him the term in any exact sense ; for as yet the industrial proletariat existed only in embryonic form, and Bunyan could not guess at the shapes and emotions of unity that would emerge out of that proletariat when consolidated. He is a writer of the transition, proletarian in that he writes from the viewpoint of the dispossessed, pre-industrialist in that he still clings to a medieval concept of reconciliation, petty-bourgeois in that he is tied down to an individualist ethic.

5

JOHN BUNYAN

He therefore sums up his age with a fullness that makes his work of enduring interest ; for the tension of all these divergent forces created in him a vehicle of expression adequate to the conflict.

What lies behind his attitude to the learning of the ' wise men ' whom he despises? Partly, the scorn of the underdog who out of his sufferings has realized a sense of human unity that transcends the meagre humanities of the ruling class. Partly, the anarchist resentment born of this scorn. Partly, a deeper sense of movements and discoveries, derived from experience, which were unsettling and disproving the eternal verities of the ' wise men '. Bacon, as well as Bunyan, was rejecting Aristotle and Plato ; and so the voices of scientist and dissident tinker merge on this point, however differently tuned and intended. The challenge to authority all along the line was, in the last analysis, working for a common end.

2

Family Crisis

BUNYAN'S father, who was born in 1602, married three times. His second wife was Margaret Bentley, a native of Elstow. He married her in 1627, and next year she bore John. In June 1644 she died.

Bunyan was now above sixteen. His mother's death was an important event, not only in the general emotional wrench and agitation that it must have caused him, but also in the events to which it led. In July his sister Margaret died. Next month his father married for the third time. We must try to estimate the effect on Bunyan of the shock of loss followed so hastily by his father's re-marriage.

The Civil War was raging. Bunyan was reaching the age when he could serve. By the end of the year either he was impressed or he had enlisted in the Parliamentary Army. This entry into the Army, at a time of civic dissension, coming so fast upon the family convulsions, could not but affect him to the depths. The extreme sensitivity of Bunyan is witnessed by every page of his autobiography *Grace Abounding*. No book has ever defined more clearly the sufferings of adolescence, the paroxysms of search

7

in a world become utterly incomprehensible. Yet in it we hear nothing of his family worries.

It is needless to say that our business here is to get beneath the form in which the search presented itself to Bunyan, and to find the personal and social bedrock on which he raised his superstructure of anxiety, terror and hope, despair and reconciliation. It was an inevitable accompaniment of Bunyan's torment that he should not be able to realize the personal and social roots of his troubles. For him his personal worries were nothing but a swarm of vile but meaningless gnats. The only meaning he could possibly have attached to them was that they were hindrances to attaining the goal of reconciliation with the Father. If he had been able to see their relation as the underlying causes of his states of mind, his whole problem would have ceased to exist.

But what he did succeed in doing was to transcribe his states of mind in terms of the contemporary religious idiom, the only idiom in which he had the chance of formulating his problems. Because of the strength of his persistence, he brought himself into the heart of the ideological storm of his age ; and he mastered that tumult to the extent of giving it a remarkably clear expression, in which the social strife and the family discord are confused and blended. The religious idiom, based on the desperate need to find and state abstractedly a ' perfect relationship ', subsumes both sources of torment.

But though Bunyan himself gives in the story of his life no direct clue to his emotional recoil from his father's quick re-marriage, we can deduce from that story the intensity of the recoil. So wildly, so irresistibly did the tempest of pang and loss burst on him—with so passionate a precision is he able to record its flux and return, the pattern of its involvement in agony and release—that we can deduce the relation of the religious sense of humiliation to the facts of his family life. He was shaken to the roots. Mother and sister were borne to rot in Elstow churchyard, and the father, forgetting them, found another bedmate. The sensitive boy felt himself miserably isolated ; and at that very moment he was torn away from the familiar village ways into the garrison life of soldiering.

He tells us that in his childhood he had suffered from terrible nightmares. Even as a child he ' did so offend the Lord ' that ' he did scare and affright me with fearful dreams and did terrify me with dreadful visions '. The day of judgement, the horrible torments of hell-fire, the presence of devils and wicked spirits, were with him as subjects of brooding from early boyhood. ' These things, I say, when I was but a child but nine or ten years old, did so distress my soul,' that in the midst of games he was liable to sudden depressions and premonitions ; and he wished to be a devil, so that by tormenting he might escape torment himself. For he imagined then that ' they were only tormentors '. Then these fancies abated somewhat and he became a ringleader of the village lads in their games and little defiances, ' all manner of vice and ungodliness ', as his later conscience called it. He says it was only chance (' a miracle of precious grace ') that he did not come into conflict with the law in these escapades and suffer ' disgrace and shame before the face of the world '.

It is clear, then, that as a boy he already had a strong streak of rebelliousness in him ; that he felt himself in collision with his environment and its values. Both the devil and god are father-figures, derived immediately from family experience but finding their deeper meaning rooted in social reality. For everything specifically human in the family relationships is born from the wider social structure enclosing the family.

The battle between devil and god thus represents a profound inner conflict, the individual refraction of social issues. It shows a violent wish to attack the authority-image and yet at the same time to find reconciliation with that image on a higher level. But the sufferer cannot reach that level of suspension, acceptance. The Father of power and order keeps on lapsing into the Devil of temptation, of unstable revolt. Bunyan's conflict led him when a boy, as it has led countless other boys, to the point of a vague lawlessness.

To such a boy the hasty re-marriage of the father could not but be a brutal blow. A powerful strengthening would be given to the devil-image, and at the same time a deeper twinge of pain would animate the impulse of renunciation. To overcome the devil, a tremendous and persistent effort of reconciliation would need to be made. That Bunyan did succeed in that effort is what constitutes his interest for us. It was the fierceness of resistance which he had to overcome within himself that communicated such clarity and urgency to *Grace Abounding* and *The Pilgrim's Progress* in the days of his conquest.

Then, since these personal conflicts did not and could not take place in a void, in a dimension of abstract human nature, Bunyan's work becomes a definition of the historical processes of his age. The pattern of his conflict and reconciliation reveals to us the pattern of the class-war in his day. For the class-war is never only a matter of antagonisms. Every advance of capitalism meant an increased socialization of the methods of production. Therefore at each stage there emerged a mirage of harmony and reconciliation as well as a deepening of irreconcilable antagonisms. The mirage, the emerging sense of a new unity, could not last ; for it was at once threatened and broken up by the intensification of social contradictions. The advance towards socialized methods went on pace by pace with a deprivation of the masses of any control or ownership of the sources of wealth. Unity and discord kept both emerging with equal energy. But though the historical process thus went on deepening its contradictions, the individuals who were living through it could imagine that they had reached a point of reconciliation. Baffled of direct social harmony, they could struggle to abstract and grasp the sense of unity which they intuited as emerging from the conflict ; then, having lifted this abstraction above the flux, they could use it as a point of vantage from which to return to the scenes of abounding discord.

This method of building an eyrie of abstraction

as an escape from contradictions which would otherwise overwhelm, is the method necessarily employed
by all thinkers in the past. The varying values of
the eyries result from the varying intensity of com-
prehension on the part of the thinkers, and the
varying richness of social experience that they em-
body.

We have noticed that we would expect a strengthening of the demoniac in Bunyan as the result of his
father's exposed sensuality. That was what happened. According to his own account he became
around this time an insensate blasphemer and swearer.
Of course there is a braggadocio of confession,
especially in testimonies of the religious saved ; and
so we have to take with a grain of salt what Bunyan
says. But after a careful scrutiny I feel convinced
that *Grace Abounding* is not only a work of the
highest sincerity, it is also the work of a man who
had an astonishing power to recall the design and
colour of past conflicts—within, of course, the
limits of the ideology in which he understood
them.

Moreover, we must remember that *Grace Abounding*,
in which he gives the detailed description of himself
as a notorious swearer and curser, was written when
there were hundreds who would read it that had
known Bunyan intimately at the period described.
He had many enemies, but no one ever impugned
any of the details in his story.

Bunyan's own writings show a strong racy sense
of the vigorous phrase and the compelling rhythm,

and he was a magnificent preacher in later life. We may reasonably guess, then, that his cursings were full of fire and passion. In the volubility of his curses he was momently releasing himself from the pressure of the god–devil conflict, finding peace by letting the devil take the whole floor. The Father as the evilly-tempting sensualist routed the Father as the image of authority become justice and mercy, become socially responsible in the highest degree imaginable at that stage of development.

In 1641 Bunyan's grandfather had died. Bunyan was then a boy of thirteen, on the edge of puberty. The death must have agitated the god–devil conflict which had appeared in the childish nightmares. The death of a father or grandfather intensifies any such struggle by throwing the son or grandson more thoroughly on his own resources, bringing him closer to the father-image in himself, the authority-image with which he must succeed in identifying himself to some extent if he is successfully to merge with the social world, the ultimate source of authority. For it cannot be too much emphasized, to correct the common psycho-analytical error, that the sanction of the father-image, though mirrored in family experience, derives at every point from the totality of social experience embodied in the cultural level of the group to which the father belongs.

Before we pass on, we will quote the following passage from the *Journal* of Bunyan's great Quaker contemporary, George Fox. It reveals, in thinly veiled form, the emotion of shame and outrage at the sensuality of the parental world. Fox is telling

of his childhood and the immediate experiences
leading up to his religious conversion :

> In my very young years I had a gravity and staidness of
> mind and spirit not usual in children ; insomuch that when
> I saw old men carry themselves lightly and wantonly towards
> each other, I had a dislike thereof raised in my heart, and
> said within myself, ' If ever I come to be a man, surely I
> shall not do so, nor be so wanton'. . . . But people being
> strangers to the covenant of life with God, they eat and
> drink to make themselves wanton with the creatures,
> devouring them upon their own lusts and living in all
> filthiness, loving foul ways, and devouring the creation ;
> and all this in the world, in the pollutions thereof, without
> God : therefore I was to shun all such.

Thus does the religious emotion feed on the sense of
irresponsibility in the adult, parental world. The
lusts which are repudiated are conceived as the essential forces of cruelty and oppression. The dark
injustices of the world are seen, not in relation to
the social whole with its distorting contradictions,
but as incidental expressions of lust. The baffled
sense of social unity flows into the imagination of a
Perfect Father.[1]

---

[1] I see no reason to doubt Bunyan's own statement that he had no
intercourse with any women but his wives. But that is not to say that his
wild sense of pollution did not have roots in physical desire. Consider
the following passages : ' In the village elemental natural forces that
may destroy the peasant farm, in the city the laws of capitalist economy
bringing on crises such as unemployment and so on, keep workers
under a threat. During childhood a boy considers his desires as just
such uncontrollable forces. . . . A child who thinks himself dirty and
wicked tends to avoid the company of other children and concentrate on
his own feelings. And such a state is considered by all religions a
necessary condition for developing a real religious feeling. Having
learned that his birth is due to his parents and their shameful and
dirty affair, the child beings to shy away from them. And religion

FAMILY CRISIS

carefully replaces the sinful earthly parents by a heavenly father and a mother who sinlessly gave birth to their son.' (Article in *Za Zdoravui Buit* (1930), cited *Red Virtue*, Ella Winters.) Also this from Bunyan's contemporary Baxter, who is telling of the types who came to him with anxiety : ' Those that were never guilty of fornication are oft cast into long and lamentable troubles by letting Satan once into their fantasies, from whence till objects are utterly distant he is hardly got out ; especially when they are guilty of voluntary active self-pollution '.

3

Soldiering

BUNYAN does not seem to have had any active experience of fighting in the Civil War. But the fact that he was for years under arms, that he was plunged from the enclosed village life into excited revolutionary ideas which swarmed in the army-discussions, that he was part of a body of men pledged in a high task, could not but leave an indelible impression.

The New Model Army that broke the King was an organization of tremendous historical significance. In it there was demonstrated for the first time that unity was possible as a popular construction on a grand scale, not only apart from feudal-religious or monarchical ideas, but in entire opposition to those ideas. Cromwell as the creator of this popular unity was the first great modern revolutionary leader.

It was he as the leader of the English people (not yet broken into the industrial class divisions) who showed that feudal absolutist concepts could be withstood and conquered. For we must understand the creed of the Divine Right of Kings as an effort on the part of the national monarch (who had supplanted the Catholic Church as the cementer of unity) to carry on the feudal ideology. It is a bad error to think this creed a Stuart invention, imported by James I into our history. Stuart policy in no way diverged basically from Tudor. There were divergences, but only such as were inevitable from the sharpening of class-conflict. All the national rulers were moving towards absolutism ; and in France and Spain they succeeded.

To the royalists the King was the sole repository of national-social unity—a slogan that had been necessary during the years of struggle against barons and Pope. Since they still looked for a semi-feudalist settlement which would fix for ever the balance of classes under the Tudors, they considered that the Parliamentarians were nothing but a pack of sectaries whose individualism could not possibly make way against the unity-symbol of kingship. Their attitude is perfectly expressed in a Civil War Ballad by a royalist :

> Come clowns, come boys, come hobble-de-hoys,
> Come females of each degree ;
> Stretch your throats, bring in your votes,
> And make good the Anarchy.
> And thus it shall go, says Alice,
> Nay, thus it shall go, says Amy ;
> Nay, thus it shall go, says Taffy, I trow,
> Nay, thus it shall go, says Jamy. . . .
> Thus from the rout who can expect
> Aught but division ;
> Since Unity doth with Monarchy
> Begin and end in One.

But these reactionaries whose idea of unity was so patriarchal, paternalist, saw only one side of the revolutionary forces. That was the individualist side which was to build bourgeois industrialism. They failed altogether to realize the other side, the new coherence resulting from the productive advance.

We can guess, then, what a shock it was for all people with patriarchal, hierarchical minds, when Cromwell built up the New Model Army. In the process of creating revolutionary discipline he created a unity which vitally combined all the progressive elements of the period. From this act came the concentration, the release of dynamic energy on which the development of the next 300 years in England proceeded. Joshua Sprigge, a contemporary, gives an excellent picture of the spirit of the Army. ' The Army was, what by example and justice, kept in good order both respectively to itself and the country : there were many of them differing in opinion, yet not in action nor business ; they all agreed to preserve the kingdom ; they prospered in their unity more than in uniformity.'

This was the Army with which Bunyan found himself identified ; and the experience of comradeship, of union in a worthy purpose, must have struck deep roots in the sensitive brooding boy of sixteen fresh from his family crisis.

He probably joined the Army in November 1644, when he had reached the regulation age of sixteen. It is important to note that his father was certainly a man of royalist sympathies, for on May 30, 1645, he had a son by his third wife christened Charles. To christen a son Charles in 1645 could mean only one thing. Therefore Bunyan's service in the parliamentary Army was in every way an act involving a sense of revolt against his father. Perhaps in the act of defiance shown in the christening we can see a retort of the father to Bunyan's soldiering. But that is only conjecture. What is sure is the antagonism between father and son.

Bedfordshire on the whole was strongly antiroyalist; it was part of the Eastern Associated Counties which were the backbone of resistance to the King. The town of Bedford was almost entirely parliamentarian. In 1648 the mayor wrote officially, ' We have not had any sequestered in our Town but a Barber, and little could be had from him; and two prebends, yielding £13/6/- '. Sir Samuel Lukes was the military leader of the county; and as governor at Newport Pagnell he had the task of keeping open the road between London and the north against possible sorties from Oxford. In October 1643 a party of royalist horse had plundered Bedford and the district, and Bunyan may have seen them galloping about.

We have records of Lukes pressing soldiers from villages near Elstow. But, pressed or volunteer, Bunyan seems to have escaped any fighting. He tells us that once he was about to go off on an expedition to besiege some place, ' but when I was just ready to go, one of the company desired to go in my room; to which, when I had consented, he took my place; and coming to the siege, as he stood sentinel, he was shot in the head with a musket-bullet, and died '.

Bunyan tells this story as an instance of the way

19

he was providentially shielded. There were later suggestions that he was present at the siege of Leicester, and this passage has been taken to refer to that siege. But Bunyan makes it clear he was not present at the siege where his substitute was shot ; and he is probably referring to some minor foray. The ' place ' may have been only a manor-house. Soldiers from Newport Pagnell were present at the siege of Leicester, but they seem to have been all dragoons, and Bunyan was of the foot.

All that we know for certain is that he served in two of Lukes's regimental companies : first under Lieutenant-Colonel Cockayn, and then under Major Boulton. He did the routine work, drill, guarding, marches on field-days, and possibly outpost duty. In a passage in *The Holy War* we get what is surely a memory of the days when the townsfolk of Newport Pagnell cheered their garrison and Bunyan shouldered his musket with pride.

They marched, they counter-marched, they opened to the right and left, they divided, and sub-divided, they closed, they wheeled, made good their front and rear with their right and left wings, and twenty things more, with that aptness, and then they were all as they were again, that they took, yea, ravished the hearts that were in Mansoul to behold it. But add to this, the handling of their arms, the management of their weapons of war, were marvellous taking to Mansoul and to me.

Sixteen or seventeen years after his soldiering, he felt himself aglow when he thought of his old garrison days.

There is reason to think that he made intellectual

contacts among the townsfolk even at this early stage. For on his first book there was the imprint of a Newport Pagnell bookseller ; and the J. G. who wrote a preface for his next book was presumably John Gibbs, the minister of Newport Pagnell. We may therefore assume that during his career in the Army Bunyan had already begun to show, even if only spasmodically, an intelligent interest in doctrinal matters ; or that he felt sufficiently identified with the town to visit and preach there after his conversion.

One fact of his soldiering is most important, since it shows that he was happy in the Army and had no wish to return to Elstow. On August 6, 1646, as Civil War was dying down after the King's decisive rout, Parliament ordered that the works at Newport Pagnell and elsewhere should be demolished ; men who were tired of service were to be disbanded, the others who volunteered for further service in Ireland were to receive a month's pay. Bunyan was one of the volunteers, and was transferred into Colonel Hammond's regiment, in Captain O'Hara's company.

That he never reached Ireland was no fault of his. The regiment was marched to Chester, and the intention was that it should go ahead to secure Dublin ; but the increasing social difficulties that had appeared after the King's defeat at Naseby and his surrender to the Scotch, were taking up all the attention of the parliamentary leaders. The Irish campaign was delayed. The regiment marched back to army headquarters in April 1647. There argument broke out.

JOHN BUNYAN

The majority of the men were tired of service and wanted their discharge. But Bunyan still chose to remain in the Army. He stayed with O'Hara and was marched back to Newport Pagnell. Mustered there on June 17, he was disbanded at the end of July.

He tells us in *Grace Abounding* of another providential escape of his. He was nearly drowned in ' a creek of the sea '. As the only time that he seems to have been near the sea was during his stay at Chester, we may take it that the accident occurred then. At some other unspecified time he was almost drowned in the Bedford River, the Ouse. Another escape he chronicles occurred when, having stunned an adder, he foolishly plucked out its fang with his fingers.

Disbanded, Bunyan perforce returned to Elstow and to tinkering. He left the brotherly ranks of the parliamentary Army, the excitement of being an actor, however humble, in great and stirring events; and became a nameless toiler once more.

He was still ' unregenerate '. Even when ' providence ' saved him from the bullet at the siege, ' I sinned still and grew more and more rebellious against God, and careless of mine own salvation '. So we may take it that however much his intellectual interests had widened, he was unconverted to an urgent sense of religion, and still indulged in oaths. That his mental horizons had widened there can be no doubt. The religious and social discussions among the soldiery could not but have fascinated him, however inarticulate and confused he was.

SOLDIERING

The Army was the centre of the turmoil of ideas which the revolution had brought into being. Under Cromwell's command the Independents came to the fore, bitter opponents of Presbyterian narrowness. In the liberty of discussion and profession that they instituted was created the tradition of intellectual and religious rights which was never thereafter to be broken in England, despite all the efforts made from time to time to do so.

Thus Baxter, one of the more conservative kind of Presbyterians, expresses the horror he felt when he encountered the Independents :

When I came to the Army among Cromwell's soldiers I found a new face of things I never dreamt of. I heard the plotting heads very hot upon that which intimated their intention to subvert both Church and State.

As always, revolutionary activity had the effect of stirring men's minds on all sides to an astonishing richness of speculation and realization. Men asked questions they had never thought of asking before ; they discovered the truth of relationships that had long lain masked. The ruling classes were perfectly aware of what was happening. As early as 1641 Edmund Waller had told Parliament how necessary was hierarchical religion for the suppression of the masses :

I look upon episcopacy as a counterscarp, or outwork, which, if it be taken by this assault of the people, and, withal, this mystery once revealed, ' That we must deny them nothing when they ask it thus in troops,' we may, in the next place, have as hard a task to defend our property, as we have lately had to recover it from the Prerogative.

JOHN BUNYAN

If, by multiplying hands and petitions, they prevail for an equality in things ecclesiastical, the next demand perhaps may be *Lex Agraria*, equality in things temporal.

And Clement Walker wrote of the Independents :

They have cast all the mysteries and secrets of government before the vulgar, and taught the soldiery and the people to look into and ravel back all governments to the first principles of nature.

The Presbyterians, representing the bourgeois proper, raged against the Independents even more than the royalists. In a petition of the Lancashire Presbyterians in 1645, there were phrases that may be quoted as typical of the hatred aroused by the Independent soldiery.

A Toleration would be the putting of a sword into a madman's hands, a cup of poison into the hands of a child, a letting loose of madmen with firebrands in their hands, an appointing a city of refuge in men's consciences for the devil to fly to, a laying of a stumbling-block before the blind, a proclaiming liberty to the wolves to come into Christ's fold to prey upon the lambs, a toleration of soul-murder (the greatest murder of all), and the establishing whereof damned souls in hell would accuse men on earth.

The spirit of inquiry was abroad everywhere, but canalized in the New Model Army to the most intense vigour and concreteness. The garrison at Newport Pagnell was not at the heart of the Independent ferment ; and Baxter says that the garrisons which he knew were far quieter than the fighting army. Still, something of the Independent spirit must have been alive at Newport Pagnell. Bunyan must have heard all kinds of questions canvassed, and his rustic notions must have had many a hard knock. That Newport Pagnell took religion seriously is shown by the fact that while Bunyan was there a Baptist preacher caused a riot by one of his sermons on infant baptism, and the town had to be placed under martial law. Sir Samuel Lukes, Bunyan's commander, was a Presbyterian, but not a bigoted one (although he was caricatured as Hudibras by the poet Butler, a royalist).

Being disbanded in 1647, Bunyan did not have any direct contact with the deepening revolutionary sense that came over large sections of the Army in 1648 and 1649. But, having so long shared the lot of the parliamentary soldiery, he must have listened to the news of the Levellers' movement with interest, if not with anything like full understanding. And he must have shared directly the excitement of the first demands made by the Army for a wider democracy. Lilburne's propaganda had already permeated the Army. In April of 1647 a spy had written that the Army was ' one Lilburne throughout and more likely to give than to receive laws '. Before Bunyan's disbandment the Army had declared itself necessary as a guard against injustice so that ' the poor commons may have a shelter and defence to secure them from oppression and violence '. That was in April. In June the Army announced its determination ' to promote such an establishment of common and equal right and freedom to the whole, as all might equally partake of but those that do, by denying the same to others or otherwise, render themselves incapable of '.

The second stage of the revolution was approaching. Lilburne was concerned with the creation of complete political democracy ; but he was not unaware, and some of his followers stressed, that such political equality must lead to economic equality. The Levellers, the leaders of the second revolution, were defeated by Cromwell. Why Cromwell had to turn against the spirit of unity he had done so much to evoke, we shall consider later. For the moment all that concerns us is the figure of Bunyan returning to his native village, turning his back on the great tumult in which he had lately played his part.

It is possible that he married while on service or immediately on disbandment ; for his first wife, whose name we do not know, was clearly not of Elstow. All we know is that in *Grace Abounding* he goes straight on after the anecdote about the siege :

Presently after this, I changed my condition into a married state, and my mercy was to light upon a wife whose father was counted godly. This woman and I, though we came together as poor as poor might be, not having so much household stuff as a dish or spoon betwixt us both, yet this she had for her part, *The Plain Man's Pathway to Heaven*, and *The Practice of Piety*, which her father had left her when he died. In these two books I should sometimes read with her, wherein I also found some things that were somewhat pleasing to me ; but all this while I met with no conviction. She also would be often telling of me what a godly man her father was, and how he would reprove and correct vice, both in his house, and amongst his neighbours ; what a strict and holy life he lived in his day, both in word and deed.

Wherefore these books with this relation, though they did not reach my heart, to awaken it about my sad and sinful state, yet they did beget within me some desires of religion. . . .

SOLDIERING

There are four points of interest about this passage. First, it makes clear that Bunyan had not known his wife's father and that she was therefore from some distant locality—so that we may presume he took her home with him. The ' presently after that ' which opens the passage suggests that the marriage took place before his return to Elstow.[1] It would have been natural that he should wish to take a wife back with him, as the mark of his full manhood and his resolution to start off entirely on his own.

Secondly, the strong praise of his wife's father, in a narrative where nothing whatever is said of his own father (except in the references to ' the meanness and inconsiderableness ' of his status), suggests emphatically that he did not place the latter in any pious category ; and as his father was still alive when *Grace Abounding* was published, the tacit contrast between the two fathers could not have been meant but to hurt.

Thirdly, when we find Bunyan still without any religious convictions, when we find him turning his thoughts to religion only after he had settled down with his wife and her manuals of piety and her devotion to her father's memory, we are inclined to ask : What had Bunyan, who showed so many signs of intellectual power in a few years' time, been doing

[1] However, as the paragraphs dealing with the narrow escapes were added in a later edition, it is hard to decide to what the phrase refers. In any event, he married in 1647 or shortly after ; and the wish to bring a ' strange ' woman home remains equally significant whatever the exact date. The woman's mental ascendancy suggests that she was older than Bunyan. Her name may have been M——, as a copy (now lost) of one of the books Bunyan mentions was reported as inscribed M. Bunyan.

with himself in the Army ? The fact that he had not been carried away by the religious arguments suggests strongly that he had other interests, possibly for the most part games and sports, possibly also problems of the secular politics which so passionately seethed in the ranks of the New Model. If such matters had partially absorbed his attention, he would certainly not have thought them worth recording when he wrote *Grace Abounding*, except under the general heading of backslidings. I do not wish to press this point, which is mere conjecture ; but what is not conjecture is the fact that he had heard, with however vague and rustic an ear, the debates on freedom which agitated the Army.

Grace Abounding has several passages where memories of discussions heard at Newport Pagnell unmistakably emerge. Bunyan puts them down to the Tempter. But such questions as ' How can you tell but that the Turks had as good scriptures to prove their Mahomet the Saviour as we have to prove our Jesus is ? ' would obviously not occur to a country lad without prompting. We hear in them the jocular voice of some freethinking soldier. ' Could I think that so many ten thousands, in so many countries and kingdoms, should be without the knowledge of the right way to heaven,' and so on. Ironic remarks that had apparently passed without thought through the young soldier's head, now revived in memory as the voice of the Tempter. Fox and Bunyan both give examples of the freethinking that was by no means so limited at this period as is usually assumed. One instance that especially impressed Bunyan occurred when he overheard 'a great man' try to seduce a girl ; she was afraid of the heavy punishments for bearing a bastard ; the man bade her tell the judge that the Holy Ghost got her with child. This ' was in Oliver's days '.

Fourthly, he makes it clear that he was mentally under the spell of his wife. It was she who took the initiative with the subject of religion ; it was she who with her pious books set him off on the trail that led to his literary masterpieces.

4

The Issues of the Revolution

WE must now pause to glance rapidly at
the basic social issues that surrounded
Bunyan. Throughout the later medieval centuries we may say that roughly the causes of King
and burgesses coincided. For what the trading and
manufacturing classes needed most of all was freedom from feudal dues and oppressions, safe com-
munications, and the breaking of the Catholic
Church's monopoly-grip over economy. Unless the
Church's grip was loosened, there was no hope of
speeding up the development from feudalism ; for
the Church, a vast European business concern with
huge land-holdings in every area, was tenacious in
preserving serfdom. It had everything to gain from
keeping feudalism intact, and needed to depress productive standards so as to continue its methods of
heaping up wealth and grabbing land. If men
started investing money in trade and industry, they
would cease thinking of the need to save their souls
by buying masses, indulgences, and so on, or by
leaving land to the Church. What suited the Church
was a settled serf-level of production, with a certain
proportion of money allotted to charity and the rest

going into the Church's coffers. Once money was diverted into expanding trade and industry, it would cease to flow to the Church.

The burgesses therefore needed to break the Church's monopoly, with its great resources of land. Their ally was the national King who was at continual loggerheads with Pope and barons. The King could not centralize and effectively impose his power while so much of the nation's money went to the Roman Church and the barons were asserting their feudal rights with the consequent multiplicity of dues, fees, and privileges, the lack of any legal uniformity, the unco-ordinated confusion of local authorities.

Thus the needs of King and burgesses both demanded a strong State-centralization.

The Wars of the Roses broke the power of the barons, and with the Tudors a strong centralizing monarchy began to function. The estates of the Church were confiscated and shared among the ruling classes, and the movement towards capitalism was speeded up. But at once the Crown came into conflict with the burgesses. For the Crown could no more tolerate a dominating class of merchants and manufacturers than the barons and the Roman Church. The Crown wanted a balance of classes ; it wanted to preserve a medieval form of hierarchy, but without the Roman Church or the barons : a project that seemed possible if one thought only in political terms.

But the economic basis on which the Crown had compacted its control was moving in the opposite direction. The history of the Tudors and Stuarts is the tale of rulers who thought that political theory could override economic needs. The Crown failed. For the very forces that had worked together to bring about the Crown's supremacy were also working to put power into the hands of the bourgeoisie. The Crown refused to recognize this fact. It continued to believe that it could impose a static system of government which would hold all the classes set and balanced by the Crown's overriding law—equity within the system.

But the medieval stability had proceeded from the fact of serfdom. The Tudors partially recognized this. They therefore tried to devise a method of tying down the labourer to his parish. But this method was at variance with the Crown's own need to go on centralizing, and it was even more at variance with the needs of the bourgeois—that is, the trading and manufacturing sections as distinct from the landed classes.

These disturbing factors were actively present from the first years of the Tudor dynasty; but it was a century and a half before they reached explosive tension. For a long while they were veiled. Throughout the sixteenth century the collaboration between the Crown and the burgesses was the main fact; in the last years of Elizabeth's reign the discords began to show themselves perturbingly. That new tension was Elizabeth's legacy to the Stuarts.

The irreconcilable nature of the needs of Crown and burgesses was laid bare from the start, when in 1487 two Acts against Depopulation were passed, one local and one general. For the bourgeoisie needed above everything else to seize the land ; and this they were proceeding to do by methods of sheer piracy, terrorism, semi-legal jugglery, and various tricks and oppressions. The Crown could not but dislike this process which was uprooting the yeomanry. The static balance of classes which the Crown required was being upset ; power was passing to one class, the bourgeoisie ; and the yeomanry, on whom the Crown relied for sturdy soldiers and for a nationally self-sufficient economy, were being dispossessed and turned into vagabonds or wretched hired workers.

Vainly throughout the sixteenth century the Crown passed law after law trying to arrest the seizure of the land by the bourgeoisie. A climax came in 1549 when the Protector Somerset made a vigorous effort to stop the depopulation. Now occurred one of the most curious episodes in our history. The peasants rose to enforce the law. Jack Ket of Norfolk was the chief leader. The Crown was faced with a dilemma. Could it support the Commons, who were doing no more than enforce the Crown's policy, against the big propertied classes ? Could the Crown stand on its own theory of equity against the classes on whose back it had ridden to power ?

The notion of national unity proved itself utterly untenable. Somerset fell. The ' rebellion ' of the peasants (which consisted of wanting the Crown's most basic legislation obeyed) was put down bloodily. The bourgeoisie had won the first round of the struggle.

The Crown attempted further compromise. While it had lost in all essentials to the propertied classes, it still brought a certain amount of pressure to bear ; and it was still serving a purpose useful to the bourgeoisie in strengthening its central control. Also, there was still uncertainty in the fight against the Roman Church, as the reign of Mary showed. That Church, with its ideology, represented the core of feudal reaction ; and that is why the national Protestant cause was able to evoke such enthusiasm. All progressive impulses were united by the need to repel Rome.

In 1593, with the Protestant cause firmly established, the inner discords of the Tudor reign once more came to a head. Elizabeth succumbed to bourgeois pressure, and for the first time for many decades there was no law enforcing tillage. Four years later Elizabeth tried to retrieve this surrender ; but another large rent had been made in the Crown's edifice of control.

Rackrenting, enclosure of common-land by the methods mentioned above, the turning out of copyholders by imposing impossible fines or charges, the rising cost of provisions (especially wheat)—these were the signs of the capitalist success. Middlemen, leasemongers, speculators, and cornerers of markets appear as increasingly important actors on the economic stage, despite all the penalties enacted against their activities. As an instance of the change of moral values, it is, however, worth pointing out that all the activities which later became the source of power and respect under capitalism were considered in these early days to be infamous and despicable, marking a man out as worse than a beast.

It was in the first full burst of capitalist energy, after the dissolution of the monasteries, we must remember, that the Bunyans lost their land.

By the time that Charles I came to the throne, the conflict of Crown and middle class had grown acute. What was most fiercely resented were the monopoly grants in trade and industry. These monopolies were an inseparable part of the absolutist methods of the Crown. If the Crown was to survive as a dominating factor in a world where it could not altogether stem the capitalist current, it must strive to control industry through monopoly corporations.

Charles failed ; but his method succeeded on the Continent. Colbert and Louis XIV carried out on a grand scale Crown-control in the sphere of economics. The effect was to cripple French industry and to create a kind of feudal bureaucracy. Not till the revolution of 1789 could the French middle class meet the English on equal terms ; and by that time England had succeeded in getting in ahead with industrialism and empire extension.

The basic issue of the Civil War in England was then as follows : Was the King to impose absolutism with its monopoly forms, or were the middle class to shake off all feudalist fetters decisively and develop towards free-trade ?

If we remember these main issues, we can understand why it was the loathed tyrant Laud who in the Star Chamber made a stand against the enclosing landlords ; the Crown was no champion of the working classes, but it had to do something with its schemes of equity to curb the power of the aggressive middle classes.

Middle class against royal prerogative. That was the basic fact. But in a class-riven society there cannot be social agitation for rights in any one section without a stimulus to all who feel wronged and oppressed. The bourgeois attack on the Crown stimulated the dispossessed peasant and the down-trodden journeyman. Thus there arose a far-reaching democratic agitation, of which the great spokesman was John Lilburne.

5

The Religious Formulation

ALTHOUGH men were well aware of the inter-
twining social and economic needs about them,
yet it was in religion that they found the final statement of the issues that beset them. We may roughly
sketch the reasons for this. At each stage of development in the productive mechanism there has
been an intensification of class-war. The control of
nature has been extended, but at the cost of divorcing
larger and larger numbers of men and women from
ownership in the sources of wealth. (Not that the
process is schematically simple ; it has eddies and
cross-currents, reversions and doublings on itself,
ceaseless ripples of class-construction and class-
collapse, ring within ring ; yet, taking the broad
historical scene, we can only generalize as above.)

Hence the discord. The control of nature draws
men together in a deeper, wider, surer bond of human
purpose ; yet the accompanying class-divisions increase the sense of stress and misery, of man against
man. Thus, in the past, the more that man pro-
gressed, the more he seemed from another aspect to
make a mess, a hell, of his world.

The sense of unity, developed by the productive

advance with its intensified socialization of method, cannot in such conditions be actualized. What would actualization mean ? It would mean that social relationships would be made as harmoniously coherent as the methods of production. But that is impossible in a class-society.

Therefore the sense of unity is abstracted. It is imagined as existing in a world where *only relationship* holds sway. In this fantasy-world man feels himself free to imagine a perfect relationship as compensation for social discord and division. But ' relationship ' cannot exist in a void. It must be abstracted from some actual form. The nearest universal form of relationship is that of child and parents ; and in class-society (which is a specific form of the patri-archal group) the child–parents relationship becomes the son–father relationship.

So it is felt that if only a perfectly concordant scheme of son–father relationship can be imagined, this abstraction will balance the loss of unity in actual life. The religious intuition thus glosses over, emotionally cements, the discord between social relationship and productive methods.

But because the sufferer, driven painfully back on himself, has been forced to abstract relationship in the personal son–father terms, the social dynamic behind the whole process is peculiarly hidden.

Take the origins of Christianity. The creation of the Roman Empire gave an enormous lift to pro-ductivity—but in terms of a slave-economy. The productive advance, linking men together on a scale without parallel, was therefore felt as a terrible mockery. The Son had been utterly sacrificed to the Father of Power. The thwarted sense of a new bond flowed into the old mystery forms of religion, burst them with an unprecedented intensity, and created Christianity.

At each crisis in the succeeding European centuries a new strength was given to the Christian images. In especial, as serf-society began to break up, there were strong efforts to re-formulate, to get a closer and more intimate sense of the relationship scheme involved. The Catholic Church resisted, ruthlessly ready to provoke any amount of bloodshed rather than to let go its vast landed estates. But the emerging forces of capitalism could not be withstood. The Church triumphed in some areas where it had particular strategic strength ; but in the northern belt the new forces smashed through.

The revolt against feudalist values took the form of Protestantism. It was not that men were unaware of the new economic compulsions. But at that stage it was not possible for them to do other than abstract the sense of unity which the productive advance involved.

They interpreted their new sense of relationship as an effort to get back to ' primitive ' Christianity ; and to an extent the analogy was correct. Their sense of crisis brought them the emotion of impending disaster, world-end, without which the Christian idiom could not be fully fused with a sense of reality. But they were unsuccessful in their efforts to discover the primitive organization of Christianity. Those efforts were made under the delusion that if they could discover and apply the primitive scheme, their troubles would all be over. What baffled them was the lack of an historical sense ; they were quite ignorant of the fact that the first requisite for a genuine reconstruction of early Christianity was a slave-society.

Abstractly considered, Protestantism is no more rational than Catholicism ; but, considered in relation to historical process, the triumph of Protestantism was a triumph for rationalism. The Calvinist might be personally as intolerant as any Catholic ; but he stood as the ideologist of forces which by carrying capitalism into free-trade were to act as powerful solvents of irrationality. In especial, we must note, the passionate hatred of the reformed Churches for any suggestion of magic in ritual showed the movement towards rational understanding of things. The Protestants rightly saw in ritualism the ideological wedge of feudal modes of thought and action. Because men could not objectify these emotions with full freedom, they seized on to trivial aspects and magnified them into central issues and causes. Thus, the Puritans were ready to die in protest against the wearing of surplices by the clergy. The emphasis on the detail seems ridiculous, till we realize what far-reaching decisions, as the antagonists rightly felt, rested on the matter of surplices or no surplices. Ultimately the question was : Shall we accept hierarchical forms, or shall we fight to actualize unity ? The surplice was the emblem of all that made for social inequality. One may compare the tremendous importance the Quakers attached

to withholding the ' hat-honour '   They would take
off their hats to no man.

We must note too that the ' creative ' period of
Protestantism came in its early centuries. By creative
I mean that at that time it acted as a definitely constructive stimulus to its professors. Though those
professors were building on economic forces that
were generated out of the collapse of feudal society,
yet they needed a banner, a sense of guiding principle,
a consecration. Thus the Protestant idiom, in which
they expressed their developing sense of unity and
mastery, was indeed a factor in bringing the unity
and mastery about. In England the first great bourgeois wave was at every point vivified by the Protestant idiom ; and this unity proceeded up to the
Civil War. After that war the inner rifts in the
bourgeoisie, the increasing pressure of a dispossessed
proletariat, destroyed the vital coherence of the
Protestant movement ; only with the lower classes
did Protestantism remain a living force, compacting
their resistance and submission till the day when
they could begin to organize for a juster society.

The medieval forms of Protestantism held in solution the discords that were to develop when the
bourgeoisie came to power. In Wiclif's work, for
instance, the attack on the religious orders for their
parasitism was one that appealed equally to plough-
man and city merchant. The core of this early
Protestantism is to be found in the hatred of all
non-producers, the wish to apply, forcibly if necessary, the command : He who does not work shall
not eat.

The first success of Protestantism under Luther showed at once the duality of application in this slogan. In the mouths of the petty-bourgeoisie it merely meant : Take the weight of the parasitic Church off our backs. In the mouths of the plough-man it meant : Let us live in a community of Christ with perfect equality. No sooner had Luther in collaboration with the local princes started off the emancipation of the petty-bourgeois than the peasants rose under Münzer, demanding communism. And Luther had to scream for bloody terrorism to sup-press them.

This dilemma has persisted ever since, and must persist till there is a classless world-society. Every bourgeois movement towards 'liberty' aroused the hopes of the labouring classes and had to be finally curtailed and betrayed, or at least diverted and obscured. Fascism is the expression of the complete betrayal, in which the bourgeoisie seek to revive feudalist methods and to make a compact with all the forces they once hated and undermined.

But to return to early capitalism : men like Luther and Calvin, expressing the outlook of the petty-bourgeois lately released from feudal burdens, were far from realizing what the release of their class por-tended. Having abstracted their sense of unity on the lines indicated as usual in each stage of religious process, they wanted to halt things at the pattern of the class-struggle emerging from the first overthrow of feudal forms. They still thought in terms of a medieval society in which prices could be pegged down to a 'just price' and where everyone would keep his place, his ' calling '. (A man's vocation in God and his calling in society were inextricably mixed.) Hence both Luther and Calvin disliked usury ; they denounced all financial parasites. They thought that the elimination of the papal monopoly merely meant that the bourgeois pattern, as they knew it, would function with increased freedom and stability ; and that only the working out of just prices was needed to keep everything set to that pattern.

In this they utterly misunderstood the dynamic nature of the class-forces they served.

Therefore there was a tendency of the early Protestant theorists to come into collision with the operation of their own class-forces. They felt morally outraged by the devices of capitalism, and outspokenly denounced them. In England we find this tendency active in the middle of the sixteenth century, when at last it had become clear what was happening. Protestants like Bishop Latimer, or Thomas Becon and Robert Crowley, courageously denounced root and branch every manifestation of capitalism ; they uncompromisingly declared that there was no possible fate for the rackrenters, enclosers, speculators, and profiteers, except damnation. Worse, they demanded social action against them. As typical of these denunciations we will take the following from *The Way to Wealth* by Robert Crowley, written shortly after the Jack Ket rebellion :

If I should demand of the poor man of the country what they think to be the cause of sedition, I know his answer. He would tell me that the great farmers, the graziers, the rich butchers, the men of law, the gentlemen, the lords, and I cannot tell who : men who have no name because they are doers in all things that any gain hangeth upon. Men without conscience. Men utterly devoid of God's fear. Yea, men that live as though there were no God at all. Men that have all in their own hands. Men that would leave nothing for others. Men that would be alone on the earth. Men that never be satisfied. Cormorants, greedy gulls, yea, men that would eat up men, women and children, are the causes of sedition.

They take our houses over our heads, they buy our grounds out of our hands, they raise our rent, they levy great (yea unreasonable) fines, they enclose our commons. No custom, no law or statute can keep them from oppressing us in such sort that we know not which way to turn to live. Very need therefore constraineth us to stand up against them. In the country we cannot tarry but we must be their slaves and labour till our hearts brast, and then they must have all. And to go to the cities we have no hope, for there we hear that these insatiable beasts have all in their hands. . . .

How were the bourgeoisie to preserve a good conscience if their own prophets turned against them in this way ? A crisis in Protestantism set in ; the simple humanity of men like Latimer and Crowley had to be crowded out ; a different ideology, one which sanctified success, had to be created.

How well the Puritan movement narrowed its basis, so as to satisfy its class-needs, is to be seen by comparing Crowley's magnificent pleas with the following passages, which represent the typical Protestantism of a century later :

Faith is a successful grace, and hath a promise of prospering. (Matthew Wren, 1660.)

You may labour in that manner as tendeth to your success and lawful gain ; you are bound to improve your master's talent. (Baxter.)

Do not tradesmen in following their vocation aim at their own advantage, do none of them glorify God thereby? (Joseph Lee.)

Grace in a poor man is grace, and 'tis beautiful, but grace in a rich man is more conspicuous, more useful. (*Sermon*, 1655.)

Calamy considers the conjunction natural when he says that both riches and piety lessened at Barnstaple after a Puritan minister was ejected in 1662. The whole emphasis has gone into the praise of success and into denunciations of idleness. As Baxter put it, ' Freeholders and Tradesmen are the strength of religion and civility in the land ; and Gentlemen and Beggars and Servile Tenants are the strength of iniquity '. This is the language of a vigorous class, not afraid of hard work, demanding the suppression of the drones, and seeing the Enemy as the lazy debauchee. But to obtain this singleness of purpose it has had to jettison the deep compassion and insight of Latimer and Crowley.

Bunyan, we must understand, developed his thought during this latter portion of the Protestant movement. He had taken part in the Civil War ; but he had also seen the deeper democratic aspirations of the Levellers proved as apparently quite futile. Returned to Elstow, he was left to his own devices, thrown back into himself, in a world where the impulse of unity had seemed to frustrate itself and where the petty-bourgeois sanctification of success was the

predominant attitude. He was forced back on his
nightmare, with heated, tormented brain.[1]

[1] James Wright in *Country Conversations* (1694) depicts, unfriendlily,
the attitude of the Puritans : ' The Parliamentarian Party were very
apt to argue the Righteousness of their Cause from the Success ; saying
that God owned his People and manifested the Justice of their under-
takings, by the many Victories which he gave them, and a great deal
of cant to that purpose '. Cf. Christian's remarks in *The Pilgrim's
Progress* : ' Some are strong, some are weak ; some have great faith,
some have little : this man was one of the weak, and therefore he went
to the wall '. The last thing Bunyan intends is to justify social injustice ;
yet the doctrine of Election cannot help providing the ideology for a
society where ' going to the wall ' is the doom of many.

6

Divided Self

BUNYAN was getting on for nineteen when he
returned home. But his was a case of prolonged adolescence ; the tensions and conflicts of his
puberty continued indefinitely. This unremitting
struggle revealed his underlying power, his refusal to
submit to the ordinary peasant standards of his
environment. Because he fought out the struggle to
the bitter end, he emerged as a man remarkably
capable of expressing his experience ; and since that
experience involved the social contradictions of his
period, his expression involved a definition of the
social pattern. But unconsciously. All Bunyan knew
was that he had saved his soul.

Puberty is a crisis of the organism, which, being
now capable of self-reproduction, must face up to
full social responsibility. In primitive communities
this fact was expressed by the ritual of initiation,
which mimicked the birth-experience, as indeed all
rites-of-transition do. When the tribe broke up and
class-society arose, the simple rite grew more and
more complex. The Egyptian and the Eleusinian
Mysteries are the classic examples of initiation rites
deepening and expanding with social content. Finally

with the advent of the Roman Empire the Mystery-idea was sharply transformed into Christianity. Behind this transformation we see the discords that had already long past invaded the Mysteries : the imageries of agricultural fertility entangled with castration acts ; the birth-mime of entry into fuller social life becoming the emblem of isolation, fear, privation. ' I weep because he is forsaken ', cried the divine sisters mourning at the bier of the mangled Osiris long before the holy women mourned at the foot of the Cross.

Class-pressure produced the complete abstraction : the individual alone with the Heavenly Father, seeking rebirth. Spiritual regeneration takes the place of the rite symbolizing adult status as a birth into the wider world of corporate activity.

The more that society is broken with contradictions, with class divisions, the more difficult becomes the passage into it of boy or girl. The crisis of puberty becomes a painful and lengthy attempt to adapt oneself to social environment. The sense of social division is inverted in the suffering consciousness as a sense of personal unworthiness, physical shame, insecurity.

As part of this inner strife there arises a need to understand, to overcome the painful confusion of the world. But—we are dealing with class-society—no full understanding is possible, no point of rest emerges, no satisfying fullness of contact. The discord appears in various abstract puzzles in which the faculty of generalization is seen impotently agitated ; the antinomies of metaphysics are the more sophisti-

cated version of these adolescent puzzles.[1] The
greater the social crisis, the greater the tendency to
probe for a new and fuller understanding ; and
where the anxious search has found its new contact
with reality, some genuine scientific discovery is
made, or a work of art is produced, or a necessary
technical adjustment is devised.

We have only to read the religious records of
Bunyan's day to see that countless men and women
of England were obsessed by the same problems as
he was. His distinction lies in the tenacity with
which he at last succeeded in disciplining his emotions
and uttering them in literary form.

As an instructive instance of the kind of desperate
struggle which Bunyan was waging, we may take this
account by a doctor of a typical case of suffering
cause by unemployment in our present England :

His injured self-esteem was so great that wherever he
went he thought people were looking at him, despising him,
sneering and laughing at him. These feelings alternated with
passionate rages in which he felt the slightest provocation
would incite him to run amok and attack people furiously
and indiscriminately. If anyone jostled him in the street,

[1] Problems which I recall distracting myself at puberty were such
as : Is space infinite? if so, how can it go on for ever? if not so, what
lies on the other side? The same with time : What happens when
time stops? but how can it go on for ever? Who made. God if God made
all things? Who made the Devil? Why can't I walk on water by
moving my feet fast enough? And I recall for years being visited by
dreams of complex moving geometrical figures, organized like music
and accompanied by a conviction of absolute certitude and exciting
discovery. Tolstoy, *Boyhood*, xix, gives an excellent summary of this
kind of thing, ' I fell into the vicious analysis of my own thoughts,
and I no longer thought about the original questions that had occupied
me, but thought what I was thinking about ', and so on.

it was a deliberate affront. A casual glance from a passer-by
was one of contempt. And all the while he held these
feelings in check. As a result he was in a state of intense
nervous tension. The slightest effort, going into the street,
or shop, or restaurant, made him sweat with fear. This
state was accompanied by a continuous profound depression,
sleeplessness, and a *compulsion to think* furiously and without
cessation on every problem of life.

This compulsion to think is the core of the
matter ; and when the sufferer is someone like Bunyan with no means of reaching a scientific understanding of reality, the subjective factor swells in
importance. The mind, seeking to relate cause and
effect, is driven into introspection ; and emotional
tensions decide the form that the attribution of
significance takes. Since the sufferer becomes the
centre of the universe, he finds an absolute meaning
in the most trivial episodes of his life ; for instance,
Bunyan saw his escape from going to the siege as a
direct interposition of the Father on his behalf.
His writings, like those of all his religious contemporaries, are full of stories of judgements on sinners.
George Fox, in his *Journal*, has a sublime arrogance
which conceives him as the centre of God's grace.
For instance, he says of the shoemaker with whom he
was put as a boy to learn the trade, ' While I was
with him, he was blessed ; but after I left him, he
broke and came to nothing '.

This attitude, making symbols of judgement out of
any odd happening, is closely related to the belief in
sympathetic magic—that one can govern life by a
gesture to which one has communicated a magical

relationship. Thus, a Quaker before Cromwell took off his cap, rent it, and said, ' So shall thy govern. ment be rent from thee and thy house '. And a Quakeress went to the Parliament with a pitcher in her hand, broke the pitcher, and declared that so would the Parliament be broken to pieces. ' Which ', says Fox, ' came to pass shortly after '. Such acts of wish-prophecy are only a hair's-breadth off the belief that the gesture can magically command the repetition of itself in the new form willed by the curse.

The sufferer is scarcely able to distinguish the world of fact from the world of emotional tensions in which he lives.

Now let us look at Bunyan in the years when the sense of division dominated him. He had settled down at his tinkering in his Elstow cottage. Opposite was a house that was once an inn, and was probably so in his day. Behind the main street, on the west, was the village green, with the ancient Moot House. On the south side stood the church ; the brass of a Benedictine abbess in it was defaced by a Puritan during these years. The church was a large building for a small village ; it had originally been the Abbey Church of a Benedictine convent. But it was the massive tower that was even more impressive. It rose detached from the church, visible from far across the level plain and standing out in dignity across the green from the village.

7

Voices

BUNYAN went on with his daily work as a tinker, travelling about the district and calling at the big houses, or he hammered away in the lean-to shed attached to his little thatched cottage. And as he hammered, his thoughts clamoured in his head. He had seen the activities of the great world, and had retired baffled of any clue ; everything had ended in confusion and frustration. Yet he had to go on thinking, seeking to make an intelligible pattern out of it all, using the only idiom of search and discovery that he knew, the Christian idiom.

The first impact of his ordered married life and his wife's simple piety was to send him to church. He 'found satisfaction for a while in the parish services, accepting parson and church-forms without question, glad to have something to take him out of himself. But soon he wore through this satisfaction. Still the uneasy voices cried on, hammering away, whispering of hell and world-end. Where was the escape, the reconciliation that would silence the voices ? His wife's trust in her father had soothed him to a certain extent, healing something of his own unrealized father-wound ; but he needed a deeper conviction.

One day as he was playing at tipcat on the green, the terror of death swooped on him. Even the sports and laughters of the village were not to be left to him by the jealous Father. He withdrew into himself more than ever ; he reluctantly retreated into his dark corner of isolation, hemmed in by the relentless voices of discord, the bass and treble of the quarrelling divided blood, out of which he could not make the concord of music. The voices quarrelled. For years he lived in wandering torment ; anxiously he revolved pattern after pattern of explanation drawn from the words of Scripture. Yet they could not save him, he could not gain conviction. There would not break in him the moment of ecstatic union that would convince him he had found and touched the core of life, the living word of unity. The inward debate of fear went on and on.

Somehow he must be able to find the scheme of relationship which would put everything right, which would give him power to transcend the division, to kill the hell-hounds which bayed across his sleep, following some blood-spoor of forgotten guilt. He staged mental dramas, tests of himself and of the truth which he grasped at. How could he know that he was on the right track ? How could he force the Father into granting a sign ? How could he trick the terrible sentinels of secrecy guarding the source of life ?

For instance, if faith could work miracles, he could find out if he had faith by trying to work a miracle. If he lacked faith, he would be manifestly damned. If he had faith, he would be able to control the

intractable world. Walking one day along the road
to Bedford, he wrestled with the wish to bid the
rain-puddles dry up. 'Puddle, be ye dry. Stone,
be thou moved.' It was a temptation, and he knew
it, and yet he could not evade the awful logic of the
devil whispering inside. If he tried and failed, he
would be lost, given over to the devil.

Dare he go on ringing the bell of the church tower?
There were five bells, and he loved to ring one of
them when the peals were wanted. The fact that he
loved the work made it seem devilish. And there
was a man, the story went, who had been struck dead
by lightning in some other church of the county,
while ringing a bell. No, Bunyan dared not go on
raising that clangour in the sky. The tower would
topple down on him and kill him. The tower of
father-pride, the erection of power, would slay him.
He dare not measure himself against it. He shivered
with castration-terror.

Yet the idea of heavenly joy-bells remained for him
the expression of full reconciliation with the Father.
The faithful pilgrims of his allegory are welcomed
into death by pealing bells; the city of Mansoul sig-
nalizes its redemption by bells of joy. But the actual
bells of earth grated and clanged with a mad call that
woke only terror.

It is of interest that George Fox too felt this horror
of the church bells as the voices of evil, commands
from the world where a vile compact had been struck:

The black earthly spirit of the priests wounded my life;
and when I heard the bell toll to call people together to
the steeple-house, it struck at my life; for it was just a

market-bell, to gather people together that the priest might set forth his wares to sale. Oh! the vast sums of money that are gotten by the trade they make of selling the Scriptures, and by their preaching, from the highest bishop to the lowest priest. . . .

And in Warwickshire, at Atherstone, when I was two miles off, the bell rung upon a market-day for a lecture, and it struck at my life. . . .

As I was walking in my chamber, the bell did ring, and it struck at my life at the very hearing of it . . .

I lifted up my head and espied three steeple-house spires, and they struck at my life. . . .

They struck at the source of life ; they castrated him from union with the true life of things ; they spoke only of hell, of a world sold to money-values.

Thus also it was with Bunyan. Underneath the direct castration-fear of father-vengeance, the fear of the murder-phallos, there is the revolt against authority which derives its sanction from the sale of flesh and blood, hiding from the truth of relationship behind the money-symbol. We mistake neurosis entirely if we probe only for physical-personal imagery, without understanding that it is the skein of social relationships which in the final analysis conditions that imagery and its effect.

So Bunyan gave up his bell-ringing. Then the voices accused him for his dancing on the green or in the Moot Hall. For a full year he fought to keep his pleasure ; then he surrendered. ' God cannot but be pleased with me now.'

The struggle went on, the voices forbidding and drawing him away from the world, counselling the entire surrender. Ah, that was what he wanted to give ; he wanted to give all of himself. But it was hard ; it was hard to abandon every little comfort and vanity ; it was harder still to be able to take one's life like a babe in one's hand and offer it up as an acceptable sacrifice to the jealous god who would detect if a jot were held back.

There were storms of terror, brain-storms of seething heat and intolerable anxiety ; and calms of exhaustion and of momentary peace. A certainty of safety, suddenly falling away ; an abyss before the thoughtless feet. ' To shake and totter under the sense of the dreadful judgment of God.' Prayer and lamentation. And the ceaseless life of the world revolving ungraspably about him, coming with the wings of doves and of ravens, a feathery softness of exultation, a leaden contraction of doubt and fear. ' Such a clogging and heat at my stomach, by reason of this my terror, that I was, especially at some times, as if my breastbone would have split in sunder ; then I thought of that concerning Judas, who, by his falling headlong, burst asunder, and all his bowels gushed out.'

For if earth was the valley of pollution, then birth was a passage through the way of filth, and the baby was the rejected dirt of the mother. What, then, was there to stop the polluted body from breaking to pieces, from bursting with its own freight of inner filth ?

This imaging of hell-torment as a fæcal birth-agony is not peculiar to Bunyan ; it is a basic form of horror. But it is strong in him :

VOICES

The hollow belly and yawning gorge of hell gave so loud
and hideous a groan (for that is the music of that place)
that it made the mountains about it totter, as if they would
fall in pieces. . . . (*Holy War.*)

Our yawning hollow-bellied place, where we are, made so
hideous and yelling a noise for joy that the mountains
that stand round about Hellgate-hill, had like to have been
shaken to pieces. (*Idem.*)

O! when they see they must shoot the gulf and throat
of hell! when they see that hell hath shut her ghastly jaws
upon them, when they shall open their eyes and find themselves within the belly and bowels of hell! Then they shall
mourn and weep and hack and gnash their teeth for
pain. . . . (*Mr. Badman.*)

It will be seen from these passages that the bell-tumult
of his fear is related to this hell-blast; and the image
of the falling hills pairs off with the image of the
falling tower.

The division in Bunyan had now reached such a
degree that he was falling into schizophrenic delusions.
The inner voice sounded in the air about him.

I was much followed by this scripture, ' Simon, Simon,
behold, Satan hath desired to have you'. And sometimes
it would sound so loud within me, yea, and as it were call
so strongly after me, that once above all the rest, I turned
my head over my shoulder, thinking verily that some
man had, behind me, called to me; being at a great distance,
methought he called so loud. . . . Methinks I hear still
with what a loud voice those words, Simon, Simon,
sounded in mine ears. . . .

When I have heard others talk of the sin against the Holy
Ghost, then would the tempter so provoke me . . . no
sin would serve but that. If it were to be committed by
speaking of such a word, then I have been as if my mouth
would have spoken that word, whether I would or no;

and in so strong a measure was this temptation upon me that often I have been ready to clap my hand under my chin, to hold my mouth from opening; and to that end also I have had thoughts at other times, to leap with my head downward, into some muck-hill hole or other, to keep my mouth from speaking.

The fear of an ' involuntary emission ' in the last passage will explain itself ; and the image of the headfirst dive into the muck-hole is related to the other images quoted above of the filth-hole of hell.

I shall here insert a brief account of an encounter of my own with someone suffering in a somewhat similar way, which I think throws some light on to the forms of divided personality as possession. A friend of mine, about seventeen years old, had taken up automatic writing with a suspended pencil ; after a while he found that he could do the writing by merely holding the pencil loosely in his hand. The ' power ' gripped him, and involuntary muscular tensions guided the pencil. It became an obsession ; and then the ' power ' began speaking directly to him as an ' inner voice '. It babbled on in his brain, and he could not stop it. At first it was very friendly ; then it turned on him, became many voices. ' They ' told him at last that they had lured him into this trap ; that they were demons, elementals, who meant never to leave him : they set him all kinds of pointless tests and tasks, which had to be carried out precisely to the time given. Then they told him they were working to break his will utterly and to make him commit suicide. He was walking with me (who did not yet know anything about the matter), and they tried to force him over a cliff that was near by. I noticed that he looked distraught and distracted. Later, when questioned, he broke down and told me what had happened. The mere act of speaking of the subject relieved him, though, he said, 'they' were hub-bubing all the while in his head, threatening him wildly for breaking the silence they had laid on him. After a few days he was talked out of his obsession and became quite normal again. The whole thing was without a fraction of a doubt a perfectly genuine 'possession'; and from what he said, it was clear that the anxiety had its roots in onanistic fears.

One more detail of Bunyan's possession requires further analysis.

I could attend upon none of the ordinances of God but with sore and great affliction. Yea, then was I most distressed with blasphemies; if I had been hearing the Word, then uncleanness, blasphemies, and despair would hold me as a captive there; if I have been reading, then, sometimes I had sudden thoughts to question all I read; sometimes my mind would be so strangely snatched away, and possessed with other things, that I have neither known, nor regarded, nor remembered so much as the sentence that but now I read.

In prayer also I have been greatly troubled at this time; sometimes I thought I should see the devil, nay, thought I have felt him, behind me, pull my clothes; he would be, also, continually at me in the time of prayer to have done; break off, make haste, you have prayed enough, and stay no longer, drawing my mind away. Sometimes, also, he would cast in such wicked thoughts as these: that I must pray to him, or for him.

As these impulses to blasphemy were bound up with

59

Bunyan's earlier indulgences in cursing and swearing, it will be worth while to examine briefly the psychology of the oath. Andrew Boorde in his *Dietary*, 1542, says, ' In all the world there is not such odible swearing as is used in England, specially among youth and children '. And elsewhere he says :

In all the world there is no region nor country that doth use more swearing than is used in England ; for a child that scarce can speak, a boy, a girl, a wench, nowadays will swear as great oaths as an old knave and an old drab. It was used, that when swearing did come up first, that he that did swear should have a fillip. ' Give that knave or drab a fillip with a club that they do stagger at it.' And then they and children would beware.

Boorde may be exaggerating in saying that the English were the worst swearers—though the strength of resistance that led them to executing Charles I might have led them to much swearing as an expression of their suppressed defiance—but he is doubtless correct in saying that he heard oaths on all sides.

Oath, curse, and blessing are closely related. Blasphemy is the oath-curse taking on a detached life of its own under increasing class-pressure. It was thus, in a way, repeating on a new level the substitution-fantasy strong in primitive forms of the oath. The Greek word for oath, ὅρκος, also meant the object sworn by, as do the words for oath in most languages. The swearer put himself in a magical relation with some object, gave it power to avenge on him the breaking of his word, transferred to it the state referred to in the oath. This transfer was often made to something eatable or drinkable ; and the compact was struck by the eating or drinking of the oath. The oath-object was a kind of hostage-self. Christ as an oath-object was especially effective ; for He was already an image of vicarious sacrifice and was eaten and drunken in the Sacrament.

The whole method of primitive thought, painfully working towards the capacity to objectify, tended to abstract every aspect of the self or the world as a distinct property or thing : a rigidity of outlook still to be found in all metaphysics. The Name was the greatest property of all, for by naming things man had made an essential act of mastery over the world. To take God's name in vain was thus to defy the whole magical scheme of things ; and in periods when one form of religious ideology was shaken, and the next form not yet stabilized, the impulse to blaspheme and swear was an act of passing defiance and release. It released because the Father was defied and yet took no vengeance, was shown to be a delusion : it also increased anxiety, for perhaps the Father was merely biding his time, hoarding his vengeance for a later explosion.

How strongly Bunyan felt the sin of blood-guilt, of having risen up (in fantasy) and struck down the jealous Father, is to be read in the following sentence : ' I was convinced that I was the slayer ; and that the avenger of blood pursued me, that I felt with great terror '.

We must also bear in mind the primitive notion that the curse is embodied in the accursed thing, so that he who transgressed became himself the curse.

In the light of these primitive fears entangling and

identifying the curser with the curse and its object, we can see the full force of the following lines from the *Handlyng Synne* of Robert of Brunne :

> If thou ever were so foolhardy
> To swear great oaths grisly,
> As we fools do all day,
> Dismember Jesu all that we may. . . .
> They scorn Jesu and upbraid His pain. . . .
> They be but God's tormentors,
> They torment Him all that they may,
> With false oaths night and day.

The swearer is a torturer of the Name, the human reality ; but this ' reality ' is already tortured (crucified on the discords of class-society). The Christian, whose reality is conceived as Christ, is, when blaspheming, a devil denying his own true-self. But the devil is the evil which has crucified Christ (that is, created class-society and greed).

The blasphemy is thus an embryonic revolutionary impulse turned in on itself and frustrated, delivering the self up to the very forces it seeks to reprobate. ' A damnable sin ', said Andrew Boorde, ' and they that use it, be possessed of the devil '. Bunyan says similarly that the liar ' has lain with and conceived it (the lie) by lying with the devil '. The frustration in the blasphemy is thus imaged as an act of outrage on oneself by the evil-father ; and since the male is thereby imaged as female, he is imaged as castrated, as reduced to final impotence by the blade of the Law.

So Bunyan went on with the misery of his search, through the changing landscape of his emotions. For his moods of lightness or despair were woven into the scenes of his daily toil. In his rare exaltations he felt so surely part of the triumphant world that it seemed he had only to utter aloud his love and the very crows that sat upon the ploughed lands would understand ; such were the dizzy gyres of unity in which he felt himself gloriously caught. And his thoughts hammered away as he sat under the hedge resting ; or looking up, he saw the face of love peering at him in a chink of light between the tiles, and his thoughts flared and merged with the blaze of flowers, the wind whistling along the lanes, the trudge of his feet marking time with the great pulse of summer.

And then the wind changed, the dusk of pain came spider-webbing the world, and all was yet to do. He was an outcast.

Thus was I always sinking, whatever I did think or do. So one day I walked to a neighbouring town, and sat down upon a settle in the street, and fell into a very deep pause about the most fearful state my sin had brought me to ; and after long musing, I lifted up my head, but methought I saw as if the sun that shineth in the heavens did grudge to give me light, and as if the very stones in the street, and tiles upon the houses, did bend themselves against me ; methought that they all combined together to banish me out of the world ; I was abhorred of them, and unfit to dwell among them, or be partaker of their benefits, because I had sinned against the Saviour. O how happy, now, was every creature over what I was ; for they stood fast and kept their stations, but I was gone and lost.

8

The Social Core

NOW we come to the consideration of the passages in *Grace Abounding* that reveal the social core of Bunyan's torment. These passages show the source of division in the outer world which was reflected in his religious conflict in personal-physical symbols of loss, fear, and pain.

They deal with two ideas : that he had sold Christ, and that, like Esau, he had sold his birthright for a mess of pottage. But to grasp the significance of these ideas to Bunyan we must take the actual passages in which he expresses them. Otherwise we cannot gauge the intensity of their conception.

First the simpler idea :

The tempter came upon me again, and that with a more grievous and dreadful temptation than before.

And that was, To sell and part with this most blessed Christ, to exchange him for the things of this life, for anything. The temptation lay upon me for the space of a year, and did follow me so continually, that I was not rid of it one day in a month, no, not sometimes one hour in many days together, unless when I was asleep.

And though in my judgement, I was persuaded that those who were once effectually in Christ, as I hoped, through his grace, I had seen myself, could never lose him for ever, for ' the land shall not be sold for ever, for the land is mine ', saith God—yet it was a continual vexation to me that I should have so much as one such thought within me against a Christ, a Jesus, that had done for me as he had done ; and yet then I had almost none others, but such blasphemous ones.

But it was neither my dislike of the thought, nor yet any desire and endeavour to resist it that in the least did shake or abate the continuation or force and strength thereof ; for it did always, in almost whatever I thought, intermix itself therewith in such sort that I could neither eat my food, stoop for a pin, chop a stick, or cast mine eye to look on this or that, but still the temptation would come, Sell Christ for this, or sell Christ for that ; sell him, sell him.

Sometimes it would run in my thoughts, not so little as a hundred times together, Sell him, sell him, sell him ; against which I may say, for whole hours together, I have been forced to stand as continually leaning and forcing my spirit against it, lest haply, before I was aware, some wicked thought might arise in my heart that might consent thereto ; and sometimes also the tempter would make me believe I had consented to it, then should I be as tortured upon a rack for whole days together.

This temptation did put me to such scares, lest I should at sometimes, I say, consent thereto and be overcome therewith, that by the very force of my mind, in labouring to gainsay and resist this wickedness, my very body also would be put into action or motion by way of pushing or thrusting with my hands or elbows, still answering as fast as the destroyer said, Sell him ; I will not, I will not, I will not, I will not ; no, not for thousands, thousands, thousands of worlds. This reckoning lest I should in the midst of these assaults set too low a value of him, even until I scarce well knew where I was or how to be composed again.

And later he returns to the theme, saying that his sin

was the greatest of all, the most bloody, for ' you have parted with Jesus, you have sold your Saviour '.

Why should the temptation come to Bunyan in this form ? He was never tempted in any way that could have brought him personally a return of money for denying Christ. No, it is the mesh of capitalist values in which he is caught : that is the source of the metaphor. For in the world of those values the selling of human lives is no metaphor : it is the basis on which society is organized. What attacks Bunyan is the cruelty of the world which is destroying his sense of human bond. It is the flaw in the conviction of unity that disquiets and obsesses him. For it is that flaw which is destroying his hope of happiness. Narrowed down into the personal, the Enemy speaks as a Tempter, the Father of filth ; but the reality of the Enemy is the insurmountable objective contradiction in the historical process as it presents itself to the suffering tinker.

And note the reference to the land as the symbol of God's enduring grace. God has promised not to sell the land. But the land of the Bunyans has been sold ; they are dispossessed, at the mercy of the world. What, then, of God's promise ? Is it a cheat ?

What the sufferer thinks is metaphor is fact ; and what he thinks is fact is metaphor. Grasp the nature of the inversion of reality in the abstraction, and these agonies of Bunyan become perfectly easy to read.

What is God's grace ? It is the sense of election, of unity. It is the *genius*, the father-potence which makes a man part of human process. The *genius* for the man of the clan was the procreative potence ; that in him which gave strength and joy. But how is the gift of potence from the Father to express itself in capitalist society ? Here, where many are called and few are chosen, how can a man be sure that he has this grace ? If Faith is a successful grace, what is the test ?

How can the lonely tinker claim grace ? God's promise abides. But God said, ' The land shall not be sold for ever '. And the land has been sold ; the yeoman has been ejected. England is full of starving vagabonds, beggars, broken men and maimed soldiers sleeping in ditches. What of the promise that the land shall never be sold ? What has happened to the land which once the homeless tilled ?

God promised the land should not be sold, yet it is sold. If there is any justice, then the dispossessed should be able in turn to sell God. But that is sin ; it is the betrayal of human unity. And that betrayal is the evil, the Judas-murder, which has caused all the trouble, which has sold the land.

What hope, then, is there for the lonely tinker who is being harried off the face of the earth ? What hope for God's people ?

Faith is a successful grace ; and yet it is the sellers of God who are the men that succeed. It is they who have sold the land ; and the land, the mother-earth, is the secure refuge. So, if the lonely tinker will also in turn agree to sell God, he will be a sharer in the land which is God's promise of security. If he sells God, he will get God back again ; he will get the land ; his faith will be a successful grace. Yet if he sells, he will break the compact of unity ; he will be damned and he will lose the land, which he has already lost. There is no hope for him. The body of life has been irredeemably sold. Yet that mangled body has been given to him as the pledge of redemption. He toils, believing the promise ; and gets nothing.

There is a sentence in the fourteenth-century *Prayer and Complaint of the Plowman to Christ* which illuminates the image of crucifixion. The working-man recounts how he and his fellows produce all the wealth of society ; they give everything to the upper classes, and get nothing in return. ' Here is a great gift of the poor man, for he gives his own body.'

The toiling masses of the Roman Empire, with their broken bodies : they were the crucified. They gave their bodies. The poor still give their bodies. In Crowley's words :

> Alas, that we should ever see
> The flesh of Christ thus bought and sold.

And the evil world whispers, ' Sell Christ '.

It is the masters who sell Christ. The poor *are* Christ.

9

The Social Core Continued

NOW let us take the Esau passages :

That scripture did seize upon my soul: ' Or profane person, as Esau, who for one morsel of meat, sold his birthright ; for ye know, how that afterward, when he would have inherited the blessing, he was rejected ; for he found no place of repentance, though he sought it carefully with tears '.

. . . concerning Esau's selling of his birthright ; for that scripture would lie all day long, all the week long, yea, all the year long in my mind, and hold me down, so that I could by no means lift up myself ; for when I would strive to turn me to this scripture, or that, for relief, still that sentence would be sounding in me, ' for ye know, how that afterward, when he would have inherited the blessing . . . he found no place of repentance, though he sought it carefully with tears '.

. . . all this while I was tossed to and fro, like the locusts, and driven from trouble to sorrow ; hearing always the sound of Esau's fall in mine ears, and of the dreadful consequences thereof.

Oh ! the combats and conflicts that I did meet with as I strove to hold by this word (' I have loved thee with an everlasting love ') ; that of Esau would fly in my face like to lightning. I should be sometimes up and down twenty times in an hour. . . .

. . . this about the sufficiency of grace, and that of Esau's parting with his birthright, would be like a pair of scales within my mind; sometimes one end would be uppermost, and sometimes again the other; according to which would be my peace or trouble.

. . . if this of grace, then was I quiet; but if that of Esau, then tormented; Lord, thought I, if both these scriptures would meet in my heart at once, I wonder which of them would get the better of me.

. . . at last, that about Esau's birthright began to wax weak and withdraw, vanish; and this about the sufficiency of grace prevailed with peace and joy.

. . . about Esau's selling his birthright . . . this was that which killed me and stood like a spear against me. . . . The birthright signified regeneration, and the blessing the eternal inheritance.

And in *The Pilgrim's Progress*, in listing the hypocrites damned Bunyan mentions Esau first. 'Such as sell their birthright; to wit, Esau; such as sell their Master, as Judas. . . .' Judas as a sinner comes second to Esau.

The first thing that strikes us about these passages is that the word ' sell ' has the same emotional meaning as it had in the temptation to sell Christ. But before we analyse the birthright-motive, it is necessary to get the coloration of the words ' pottage ' and ' birthright ' as Bunyan felt it.

Pottage was the common food of the poor. ' Only a mess of plain frugal country pottage was always sufficient for him ', says Taylor the Water-poet in one of his pamphlets. But it was also a slang term for the Book of Common Prayer:

As the sectaries increased, so did their insolence increase. I have myself been in London when they have on Lords-days stood at the church doors while the Common Prayer was reading, saying, ' We must stay till he is out of his pottage '. (*Baxter*.)

Rushing into the Church with pistols and drawn swords, they affrighted the whole congregation, wounded one of them, who soon after died, and shot another dead on the place ; and withal declared that could they get the Doctor, they would chop the rogue as small as herbs to the pot, for suffering Pottage (for by that name they usually styled the Book of Common Prayer) to be read in the Church ; others said they would squeeze the Pope out of his belly.

. . . They sat with their hats on in the church, made a noise to drown the curate's voice, called out aloud to him to come out of his calves-coop and make an end of his Pottage. After which they seized the Bible and were going to tear it in pieces ; but being prevented, they exchanged it for the Common Prayer Book which they carried through the street in triumph ; and at last tore out the leaves of it ; some of which they trod under their feet, some they pist upon, and others they fixed upon the tops of their clubs. (*Walker.*)

' The antichristian pottage.' [*Phrase quoted by Baxter.*]

And seeing that Liberty's gained by the Scots,
Let Englishmen seek for it, it may be their lots.
Then join hands together and fear not their wrath
But cry down the prelates and spew out their broth.
[*Popular song, about 1642 ; the ' prelates' broth '
is the mess of pottage.*]

The felt-maker and saucy stable groom
Will dare to perch into the preacher's room,
Each ignorant, do of the Spirit boast,
And prating fools brag of the Holy Ghost,
When ignoramus will his teachers teach
And sowgelders and cobblers dare to preach ;
This shows men's wits are monstrously disguised
Or that the country is antipodized.
When holy common prayer is by the rabble
Accounted porridge and unfruitful babble.   (*Taylor.*)

I give these passages, partly because they show how strongly the notion of Esau's pottage as the symbol of selling oneself was fixed in the popular mind ; partly because of the picture they give of the violence to which religious earnestness among the people often led in these years.

The Book of Common Prayer represented the tyranny of the Crown. Rightly, as an expression of hierarchical religion, it was considered to be reactionary, heading for papistry and feudalism. To come to terms with the hated oppressors meant to accept the Book of Common Prayer. That was the first and simplest meaning of the phrase about Esau to Bunyan : to strike a bargain with iniquity, to accept the terms of the world's masters, to move backward to feudalism instead of striking forward into the Protestant formulation, the conviction of grace. And so we see why the church bells became hell's bells ; they summoned men to the ' mess of pottage '.

Yet the parable also meant much more than this to Bunyan. For otherwise it would not have come for him into such violent collision with the texts about grace. He felt in it a menace, which shook his conviction of grace to the roots. To understand why this was so, we must grasp the overtones and undertones of the word ' birthright ' to a man of Bunyan's generation. There was no other word which held so revolutionary a political significance as that word. To make this clear we shall need several quotations, as the only way we can revive the associations of a word that played a key-part at a certain moment of time, is by considering utterances made by men who used it with all the heat and force of meaning it then had for them.

We shall at once be struck by the curious fact that ' birthright ', the word which torments Bunyan in his effort to find a religious formulation for his world, is the very word that provided the basic emotional stimulus of the Lilburnean revolutionaries.

Lilburne had been a leader in the fight against oppression ever since as a lad of twenty he had been gagged in the pillory because he would not stop addressing the people. As we have seen, his influence in the Army was already overwhelming before Bunyan was disbanded. The soldiers, another report said later, read his books as if they were the law of England. Lilburne's thought is aptly summarized by the title of one of his chief books : *England's Birthright justified against all arbitrary usurpation, whether regal or parliamentary, or under what vizor soever.* This book was printed in 1645, and was the key-book to the advancing wave of democratic emotion that threatened to go entirely beyond the bourgeois objective and to demand real freedom for all. In this book, which was widely read throughout the Army, Lilburne pointed out that the episcopalian or hierarchical Church was intimately bound up with the economic monopoly-forms that absolutism was developing, ' the one helping the other to enslave the people '.

In basing his demand for a revolutionary reconstruction of society on the notion that in the present state of things men had been cheated out of their ' birthright ', Lilburne was bringing to a head the idiom of protest that the earlier Puritans such as

Crowley had created. Crowley told the rich they were the murderers of the poor, ' for you have their inheritance '. In *An Information and Petition* he says, ' The whole earth therefore (by birthright) belongeth to the children of men. They are all inheritors thereof indifferently by nature '. And Francis Trigge, in attacking Enclosures in 1604, declares :

Hereby the poor cannot enjoy their ancient Commons and Liberties. And this cankered Thorn also devoureth God's people, which is his inheritance, as the Psalm teacheth us, Ask of me (saith God) I will give thee the people for thine inheritance, &c. and the uttermost parts of the earth for thy possession. Enclosers to maintain their own inheritance do make no conscience to impair this inheritance. . . . Must they impair the Lord's inheritance to maintain their estates ? . . . Nay, they had better never been born than to exalt themselves to impair his inheritance. . . . These Enclosers go about to make England as barbarous and as weak in this respect [lack of yeomen] as other nations. . . . They kill poor men's hearts . . . so that now they are forlorn, having no joy to live in the world. (*Petition.*)

Indeed the poor men were forlorn, as we have seen in the case of the Elstow tinker, having no joy to live in the world.

The extent that this idiom of protest had been spread by Lilburne's propaganda may be measured by the following examples. The first is from a weekly news-sheet of 1649. Custom, says the writer, had so dulled men into an acceptance of Tyranny that Tyranny ' at last became so customary to the vulgar it seemed most natural (the only reason why the people at this time are so ignorant of their equal

Birthright, their only Freedom) '. By ' equal Birthright ' this writer meant complete economic as well
as political freedom ; his paper *The Moderate* consis-
tently pointed out, week after week, that private
property, private ownership of the sources of wealth,
was the cause of all the troubles from which people
socially suffered.

Here is Winstanley's statement when arrested for
trying to start a communist colony :

> And is this not slavery, say the people, that though there
> be land enough in England to maintain ten times as many
> people as are in it, yet some must beg of their brethren,
> or work in hard drudgery for day wages for them, or starve,
> or steal, and so be hanged out of the way, as men not fit
> to live on the earth?
> Before they are suffered to plant the waste land for a
> livelihood, they must pay rent to their brethren for it.
> Well, this is the burden the Creation groans under ; and
> the subjects (so-called) have not their Birthright Freedom
> granted them from their brethren, who hold it from them
> by club law, but not by righteousness.

Note the contrast drawn between the perfect law of
liberty (the common birthright) and the rule of
imposed law. It is this sense of contrast and revolt
which is basic to all creative Christianity, from Paul
to Wesley.

And here are a few utterances from the leaders of
the Army at the Putney Army Council meetings, end
of October 1647 :

> *Mr. Pettus:* We judge that all inhabitants that have not
> lost their birthright should have an equal voice in
> Elections.

JOHN BUNYAN

Col. Rainsborough (speaking in defence of ' the just and equitable rights that the people of England are born to ') : I think that the law of the land in this thing private property is the most tyrannical law under heaven, and I would fain know what we have fought for. The thing that I am unsatisfied is how it comes about that there is such a property in some freeborn Englishmen and not in others.

. . . that which enslaves the people of England that they should be bound by laws in which they have no voice at all.

Mr. Wildman : Our cause is to be acknowledged thus, that we have been under slavery. That's acknowledged by all. Our very laws were made by our Conqueror. Every person in England hath as clear a right to elect his Representative as the greatest person in England.

. . . Whether any person can justly be bound by law, who does not give his consent that such persons shall make laws for him.

Saxby : We have engaged in this kingdom and ventured our lives, and it was all for this : to recover our birthright and privileges as Englishmen.

We had little property in this kingdom as to our estates, yet we had a birthright.

I wonder we were so much deceived. If we had not a right to the kingdom, we were mere mercenary soldiers.

I am resolved to give my birthright to none. Whatsoever may come in the way and be thought, I will give it to none.

I think the poor and meaner of this kingdom (I speak as in that relation in which they are) have been the means of the preservation of the kingdom.

Capt. Clarke : If every man hath this property of Election to choose those whom you think fit, you fear it may beget inconveniency.

Capt. Awdeley: I would die in any place in England, in asserting that it is the right of every freeborn man to elect.

Read carefully these words. In them you hear the actual voices of the parliamentary Army. By a fortunate chance Clarke took extensive notes of the Putney conversations ; and in these speeches we come closer to the reality of the day than we could possibly do by any other means.[1]

These are the voices that Bunyan heard about him in the Army. Then he was a distracted lad, inarticulate, earnest, still half-stupefied with his personal crisis. But these were the voices he heard ; and they stirred and woke yearnings and resolutions in him, burst in excitements that he could not control, agitated him and then seemed to pass away, leaving him the prey once more of his unresolved personal discords. But the impression remained, giving the village lad surmises and intimations of larger issues, great questions and valiant arguments.

Consider some of the implications of this idiom of revolt. Trigge pointed out, building on Crowley's indignant compassion, that God's inheritance was the people ; therefore all who marred the concord of the human bond were men who bought and sold God's inheritance. They sold Christ. Out of this emotion came George Fox's passionate hatred of organized religion, its mass-priests and its steeple-houses. The

[1] So strong was the contemporary sense of common social and economic rights as a Birthright that even when Rowland Hill wrote a pamphlet on postal reform, aimed at making the post a *common* possession, he called his work *A Penny Post, or a vindication of the Liberty and Birthright of every Englishman.*

Church of Christ were the living men and women united in a common purpose of love and work.

He asked me what a church was? I told him the Church was the pillar and ground of Truth, made up of living stones, living members, a spiritual household, which Christ was the head of; but He was not the head of a mixed multitude, or of an old house made up of lime, stones, and wood. . . .

Dost thou call the steeple-house the church? The church is the people, whom God hath purchased with his blood, and not the house.

Not a mixed multitude. Not a hierarchical edifice of classes, oppressing and oppressed; but a body of unity. Fox here has the intuition of a classless society. His cry against the world was, ' You have no unity in you '.

And take the words of blunt Saxby at Putney. Here speaks the dilemma of the men who had fought in the war for freedom. Unless they were acting as free men, they were nothing but the paid hirelings of the grandees. And if they were free men, then they and their like must have as much voice as the grandees in governing England.

And they were crushed by the grandees. So they were only paid hirelings. They had sold themselves to bloodguilt. ' I stood ', wrote Bunyan, ' with the avenger of blood at my heels, trembling at their gate for deliverance, also with a thousand fears and mistrusts, I doubted they would shut me out for ever '. What is he expressing, with this sense of bloodguilt and his horror of selling Christ, but the emotion which Saxby puts in simple terms of fact? In

Bunyan this emotion has been cut off from the basis in fact, driven back upon itself, swollen and fed with unrealized pang and fear, till it takes on a life of its own, a monstrous life threatening Bunyan night and day with the penalty of his failure.

Birthright and blessing have been lost. These signified, said Bunyan, regeneration and eternal-inheritance. ' Regeneration ' was, we saw, the abstracted form of the initiation-rite ; its mere existence revealed that the boy could not pass directly and painlessly into adult life, adapting himself to a comprehensible dimension of thought and act. So Bunyan's phrase means that no longer can the individual find harmony with his environment ; he cannot pass at puberty into a world where he has his brotherly part to play. He has lost his part in the world, his social inheritance. He is lost, cut off.

The eternal-inheritance is the symbol of that security which possession of the land granted. (At least 8·45 per cent. of Bedfordshire was enclosed between 1455 and 1607—a large proportion when we remember that in those days the cultivated area in England was much smaller than in the next centuries.) The Bunyans had lost their part in God's promise, the land ; they were cut off from God's inheritance, the human bond. Not that they would gain promise and inheritance back if they were to get hold of a piece of land again. For security did not come from merely holding the land ; it came from holding the land in terms of the social bond. That bond had been broken.

To the sufferer it seemed as if the fragment of full

clan-life represented by the common-lands had been fulfilled with a perfect sense of union and harmony. For he is using the unity-sense created by the new productive advance to evaluate that which he has lost.

He has lost the land, the earth of unity. ' I wonder we were so much deceived.' [1] Political activity has proved a snare and a delusion, leaving only the frantic sense of blood-guilt. Yet ' I am resolved to give my birthright to none '. How can that emotion survive when it has been made finally clear that the poor and meaner of this kingdom are dispossessed ; that freedom for them is shut definitely outside the horizon of time ? If the poor stupefied sufferer, who has listened with uncomprehending, obstinate exaltation, is determined not to surrender, even now when all has been taken from him, how is he to manifest his determination not to sell the birthright ?

Sell, sell, whispers the devil to the poor man who has nothing to sell. Nothing except his own body : the toiling, broken body which is Christ crucified. Sell Christ.

To live, he has to sell his body, his labour-power. But he will not sell his imagination of unity. Selling Christ, he is the only one who will not sell Christ.

---

[1] The mood of disillusion that had come over the soldiers who fought against the King is further clearly stated by Winstanley in 1649 : ' Will not this blast our honour, and make all monarchical members laugh in their sleeves to see the government of our Commonwealth still built upon the kingly laws and principles ? I have asked divers soldiers what they fought for. They answered they could not tell, and it is very true indeed they cannot tell, if the monarchical law is established without reformation.' And remember that Winstanley is making this protest as a man conscious that the *land* has been stolen from the people.

Whereas the masters, who feed on the blood and sweat of Christ, are those who sell Christ, are those who sell their souls to the devil of greed.

The slave desired money that he might buy his freedom ; but there was no means of buying the unity that he coveted as only true freedom. Therefore Christ crucified ' purchased ' the slave's redemption. The slave still gave his broken body, but he imagined unity.[1]

Bunyan, the poor sufferer, who was guiltless of any of the oppressions that rent England, felt himself as the one tempted to sell Christ. In the inner drama of the lost soul the facts are inverted. Bunyan is a poor man, dispossessed, bought and sold. So he is the one tempted to sell. And he overcomes the temptation. Thereby he feels that he has risen above the seller and buyer. It is an emotional compensation. But it is more than that. In it the future speaks. By his repudiation of the tempter Bunyan intuits the day when no man shall be bought and sold. He surrenders to the world, seeing it irresistible ; but at the same time he is absorbed in the conviction of unity, and that is his triumph, that is the sweetness flowing from his wounds.

So we can now understand why he felt the Esau-

---

[1] Note the way in which the Son makes his claim on Mansoul in *The Holy War*. 'I am my Father's heir, his first-born, and the only delight of his heart. I am therefore come up against thee in mine own right, even to recover mine own inheritance out of thine hand. . . . Nor have I been forced, by playing the bankrupt, to sell, or to set to sale to thee, my beloved town of Mansoul. . . . Mansoul is mine by right of purchase. . . . Thou art a usurper, a tyrant and traitor in thy holding possession thereof.' The purchase was : 'I gave body for body, soul for soul, and life for life, blood for blood.'

parable to be in such violent opposition to his feeling of grace, of election. The parable was based on the fact that the birthright had been stolen ; unity was broken, and the emblem of that breaking was the land which had been stolen from the people. The sense of evil, of loss, became an accusation, though Bunyan himself and his fellows were the last who could be accused of responsibility for capitalism. Yet revolutionary hopes had burned high—and Bunyan had felt them in however diffused and incoherent a fashion —so that the return to the usual life of the oppressed poor seemed a betrayal of the human bond. ' I wonder we were so much deceived. If we had not a right to the kingdom, we were mere mercenary soldiers.'

The poor tinker cannot unravel that dilemma ; but he feels it acutely. His effort to understand is based on the wish to act purposefully. He wants to redeem the birthright. He wants the land.

There were two ways of getting the land. One was the way of revolutionary action, the way of Lilburne and Rainsborough and the others, the way of Thompson and his men who died in Oxfordshire at the call of the Birthright. But that way it seemed had led to utter frustration. The men who tried it were scattered or slain ; and the guilt of their blood was on the heads of those who had not rallied to their trumpets of deliverance. Even Winstanley and his Diggers were crushed when in April of that year they set up a communist colony on St. George's Hill, meaning to do no more than peaceably till waste common-lands and convert the rest of England by an example of brotherly union.

THE SOCIAL CORE CONTINUED

The oppressors had won. The oppressors had the land. Here, then, lay the second way. One could join in with the oppressors. One could accept capitalism and join in the money-scramble. With luck or persistent scheming one might get enough money to become a landowner. This was the way of selling Christ, selling God's inheritance, the people.

That was the choice. Not that it presented itself in that form to Bunyan. It presented itself in terms of spiritual conflict, ideological debates. But the choice between Lilburne's way and the way of the capitalist was what underlay the whole debate. For if Bunyan was to claim grace, he claimed God's election. Faith was a successful grace. The notion of grace was partly a compensation for the lack of unity, partly an ideological disguise of the fact that in class-society many are called and few chosen. The masses go under ; a few men are on top. This becomes in abstraction the notion that only a few are saved, the rest are doomed to loss by laws of eternal doom—that is, by the blind operation of class-forces.

Bunyan was struggling to accept this Calvinist notion of grace ; for by it he would be enabled to reconcile himself to the world in which he inescapably found himself. Yet every time he advanced towards it, the Esau-parable intervened, accusing him of being ready to sell his birthright.

It will be clear, then, the belief in grace or election was not merely an excuse for capitalist practices, a short cut to good conscience—though it did have that effect. It was in essence an effort to reconcile the sufferer to a world in which capitalist values could not be evaded. Calvin, its greatest formulator, had a personal dislike of capitalist financial practice ; he was seeking to create an ideology, within the limits of Christian dogma, which would make it possible for men to maintain a belief in the Father while living in a capitalist society. But by enabling them thus to reconcile themselves to such an existence, he also provided the ideology which could be turned into a sanctification of capitalism.

The last thing that Bunyan wants to do is to become a capitalist. But he wants to find some way of reconciling himself to existence under capitalism ; and that is why his prolonged inner conflict centred round the issues of grace and birthright.

It was not till he was able to surrender hope of the birthright that he could achieve the desired conviction of grace. In *Grace Abounding* we can trace the steps by which he loosened his grip on worldly hope. At each step he grew more sure that his inheritance, his salvation, lay off the earth. That is, under the religious formulations, he was tearing out of himself all the tendrils of emotion that led back to political action, to the world where men spoke as Saxby spoke at Putney. When at last he felt utterly broken, when the Esau-text no longer had power to torment him, he was able to make the final step into the conviction of grace.

That moment came when he was one day ' passing in the field ' in a tremulously distraught state. Suddenly there thudded into his head, *Thy righteousness is in heaven* ; and he had a vision of Christ at God's right hand. At last he had got what he wanted. He saw

' that it was not my good frame of mind that made my righteousness better, nor yet my bad frame of mind that made my righteousness worse ; for my righteousness was Jesus Christ, the same yesterday, to-day, and for ever '.

He declares, ' Now did my chains fall off my legs indeed. . . . My temptations also fled away, so that from that time those dreadful scriptures of God left off to trouble me ; now went I also home rejoicing, for the grace and love of God '. His troubles were not yet finished, but he had made the decisive step.

That is, he had at last succeeded in abstracting his sense of justice and mercy. He no longer blamed the world (mirrored in his own veering moods) for failing to live up to its professions of humanity, for failing to actualize the sense of unity which he intuited ; he could accept the weaknesses in himself that made him fall short of ' Christ '—the shortcomings of the world that could not actualize unity. And he had managed to attain this state of acceptance of things as they were, by abstracting the sense of unity which they affronted. Unity was in heaven—in the future : cut off from all possibility of actualization. Beyond death : beyond Bunyan's death and the dissolution of the social forces which he now felt could not be challenged. Having finally decided that unity was ' in heaven ', he felt joyful, relieved from the terrible texts about Esau and the Birthright. For he was free now to make the best of a bad job on earth, spreading the evangel of unity in the only terms effective for his age, no longer tormented into paralysis by the contrast between that evangel and the ' bad frame ' of things.

JOHN BUNYAN

It may be asked why he could not face the issues in the terms in which I state them ; why he could not say ' in an earthly future ' instead of ' in heaven '. To ask this question is to misunderstand the whole nature of rationality. At every stage in human development the central issue is the sense of wholes, unity ; and until the science of dialectics had been created (following the enormous lift and centralization given to productivity by industrial capitalism), there was no means of bringing the sense of unity into fully conscious relation with the material world. Hence unity was always abstracted in some shape or form. We may note in passing how *Grace Abounding* gives us the clue to all platonist constructions. The crisis through which Bunyan went as the result of the social pressures of the Civil War is paralleled by the crisis through which Plato went when Athens was taken by the Spartans and the world seemed given up to fratricidal commerce and war. The way that Bunyan obtained relief by lodging his concept of righteousness in heaven is closely related to the way in which Plato found relief by lodging his concept of justice, and with it all other Forms, outside space and time.

In Bunyan this process had extreme interest, for his power of grasping the ideological issues led him to write the masterpiece of *Grace Abounding*. But the process, in simple or complex form according to the resistances encountered, is common to all religious experience. ' Oh, the brokenness that was amongst them in the flowings of life ', says Fox. The conviction of absolute loss is the necessary first step to the conviction of grace ; but ' absolute loss ' will in every age bear on inspection the pattern of the age's social content. It is not loss in a void ; and as we have seen, Bunyan's sense of loss expresses itself in terms of his age's discords, not of any abstract human-nature.

Before we leave this section, there are some other points to be mentioned. First, the prominence of land as the symbol of social wealth. In pre-industrial days the land was incomparably the greatest source of wealth. In the speech of Waller's quoted earlier, the confiscation that is feared by the ruling class is confiscation of land, *Lex Agraria.* Though Harrington, the bourgeois theorist of the Commonwealth, could say, ' Dominion is Property real or personal : that is to say, in lands or in money and goods ', it was primarily of land that he treated as the source of wealth and power in his Oceana. (We may note in passing that Harrington's one point of greatness is his realization that Power is always a derivation from Property, that political forms derive from class-tensions.)

It was indeed this fact that land was still the prime source of wealth that defeated the Levellers. For, as the experience of antiquity has shown, the sharing out of land can never produce an enduring equality as long as the class-structure of society remains. If the land is shared, all that happens is the starting of capitalism afresh, with a different shuffling of units.[1] Yet the

---

[1] However, one must emphasize that the shuffling of units is an essential part of development in class-society. The redistribution of land that went on during the Civil War was enormous. Fines, confiscations, levies, loss of rents, fall in land-values, crippled large sections of

revolutionary Levellers could have done little more, if they had succeeded, than make an attempt to give every family a small farm. Only when industry has advanced to the point where a vast extension of socialized methods has been adopted, does communism become a practicable system. That is why Cromwell, standing for the petty-bourgeois demands that industry should be allowed to develop, was able to defeat the Levellers, who were animated by a sense of human equality ahead of their times.

Secondly, we may note how the idea that man could claim a natural birthright was disintegrating the religious concept. One of the petitions of the London journeymen, seeking to democratize the Companies, shows that there had arisen a rooted belief that in some primitive past had existed a social form with a perfect harmony of relationships. (This was partly a vague memory of clan-life, but clan-life imagined in terms of the needs of class-society.) Somehow this perfect social form could be revived. Then there would be perfect harmony between the people and those to whom they delegated power. (An intuition of the soviet form.)

It will be evident that this contemporary agitation on the question of Elections—instances of it can also be seen in the Putney speeches already quoted—was a contributory element to the importance assumed by Election in religious ideology. Election had indeed become a momentous issue for the godly in 1653 when

---

the former landowners, and the merchant-class greedily bought up land wherever possible. This change in landownership expressed the class-shift of power.

it was the Congregationalist Churches, such as the one to which Bunyan belonged, that had the right to nominate the members of Parliament. The essence of the religious notion of Election is to be found in the wish to submit to the blind operation of irresistible class-forces, as we have seen ; but as that operation also involves the question of delegation of power, the religious sense of Election is in part an abstraction from the social forms of election or delegation. The masters are chosen, or choose their nominees, to assume power ; the religiously-chosen are those picked out to receive the father-gift of grace.

How close the religious emotion of Election could come to its social bases is to be seen in the following passage from the speech that Cromwell delivered to the 1653 Parliament. Cromwell here explicitly identifies spiritual election and social-political election :

If it were a time to compare your standing with those that have been called by the Suffrages of the People—which who can tell how soon God may fit the People for such a thing? None can desire it more than I ! Would all were the Lord's People ; as it was said, Would all the Lord's People were Prophets.   I would all were fit to be called. It ought to be the longing of our hearts to see men brought to own the Interest of Jesus Christ. . . . So that they may see you love them ; you lay yourselves out, time and spirits, for them ! is not this the likeliest way to bring them to their liberties ?

(Note his interjected cry, bewildered but sincere, that he cannot see the basis on which democratic activity is to be built at this historical stage, and his fierce declaration that it is democracy he desires. We shall later have to consider this dilemma of Cromwell's.)

Carlyle in his commentary sees the peculiar ideological confusion of this speech. He notes that Cromwell takes the ability to prophesy as meaning ' fit to sit in Parliament and make Laws ', and comments that to bring men to ' own the interest of Jesus Christ ' and to realize ' their liberties ' means for Cromwell ' to make them free by being servants of God ; free and fit to elect for Parliament '

One has so often to work by means of indirect clues and emotional associations to find the factual basis underlying the abstraction, that one is astonished when one finds, as in this passage from Cromwell, the veil wearing so thin that the connexion is confessed. Cromwell identifies religious calling and social activity, spiritual election and social delegation.

' Nature ' used as a moral or social counter always refers to the sense of expanding human bond derived from the productive advance and felt to be in conflict with the rigid morality of the preceding stage. When Rousseau said that feudalism was ' contrary to nature ', he meant that it was contrary to the sense of human freedom he felt—quite unaware that that sense did not come from any abstract Nature, but came from the very industrial advance that he disliked. ' Nature ' thus holds in solution the conflict between the past stage and the superseding stage, and the conflict between the methods and relationships in the latter.

In a Hertfordshire petition against Tithes, 1647, we find a sentence which admirably shows how the religious idiom was yielding to the rational in this matter of birthright : ' How stands it with the moral law of God, and the law of nature, or sound natural reason . . . ? '

So far we have treated Bunyan's abstraction of the Birthright, reaching down to the concrete elements underneath by analysing his *terms* for their basic emotional associations at that point of time. But there is a passage in *The Pilgrim's Progress* where Bunyan himself admits, definitely though incompletely, the social basis which we have been discussing. The reason why he is able to do so later in life, whereas at the time of *Grace Abounding* he felt enclosed by the purely theological interpretation, is doubtless to be found in the fact that as time went on the intensity of the conflict between Birthright and Grace died away ; he was so much absorbed in his pastoral, preaching, and literary work that he could afford to let a wedge of direct application intrude. For he could no longer be thrown off his balance of reconciliation.

The passage in question occurs in a conversation between Hopeful and Christian. They are discussing Little-faith, who has been waylaid by robbers after his purse. They compare Little-faith with Esau. ' Esau's belly was his god.' Esau is thus one of the Devourers, far below Little-faith, who, with all his faults, was set on higher things. Esau is the type of man who cannot see farther than the immediate lust ; he will sell himself and anything else to satisfy his greed. He is of those ' faithless ones ', who ' for carnal lusts pawn or mortgage or sell what they have, and themselves to boot '. Whereas those who have faith, however little, cannot act in this way. Esau here appears as identical with the cormorants and greedy gulls of Crowley's picture. (Esau the loser is confounded with the brute-blind forces that engulf him—just as we saw Bunyan, the guiltless, torment himself with the charge of selling Christ.)

The image of the lost birthright persisted till the end of the enclosures. Thus the poet Clare in the early nineteenth century, in a poem cursing the Enclosers, begins, ' Then came enclosure—ruin was its guide ', and ends, '. . . who glut their vile un-satiated maws, And freedom's birthright from the weak devour '.

Indeed, so obvious is the relation between the Esau-parable and the loss of the land, that I give another instance of its use by a writer who could not possibly have had Bunyan in mind ; the subject is the early enclosures of the sixteenth century :

The simple people, encouraged with the prospect of seeing better days, acquiesced in the spoliation, and saw, when too late, how they had been deprived of their birth-right without the poor consolation of the ' mess of pottage ' which is usually the reward of men who barter away that which their fathers have painfully gained.[1]

[1] J. M. Cooper, in intro. to *Select Works of Rob. Crowley*, 1872. The phrase maintains its force. While writing this chapter, I noticed the following in a newspaper article on Lord Snowden's death : ' He was accused of an act of gross treachery, of selling his soul for a mess of pottage '. (*News Chronicle.*) And this (*Reynolds News*, 23/5/37) : ' So he sold his corporate birthright for a mess of private pottage '. And at the same time re-reading Dickens's *Bleak House*, I struck : ' Harold Skimpole loves to see the sun shine ; loves to hear the wind blow ;

THE SOCIAL CORE CONTINUED

The following two passages will show the Birthright concept at important stages of its development. The first is from Jonathan Swift's fourth of the Drapier Letters, which was written as an appeal and call-to-courage to a people crushed by continued oppression, in response to the Government's threat to invoke military force :

A people long used to Hardships, lose by Degrees the very Notion of Liberty, they look upon themselves as Creatures of Mercy, and that all Impositions laid on them by a stronger Hand, are, in the Phrase of the Report, Legal and Obligatory. Hence proceeds that Poverty and Lowness of Spirit, to which a Kingdom may be subject as well as a Particular Person. And when Esau came fainting from the Field at the Point to Die, it is no wonder that he sold his Birth-Right for a Mess of Pottage.

Here the parable is coming into something like full social consciousness. What is the selling of the Birthright, which makes one brother richer than another, but the emergence of Classes ? The dispossessed, awakening to a sense of unjust deprivation and outrage, asks in bewilderment what strange and cruel bargain has he struck. How is it that one man has gained and another lost ? How have Classes come into existence when all men are Brothers ?

This sense of widening brotherhood derives from the potential in the productive advance, which creates a sense of unity that it cannot satisfy while classes

loves to watch the changing lights and shadows ; loves to watch the birds, those choristers in Nature's great cathedral. And does it not seem to me that I am about to deprive Harold Skimpole of his share in such possessions, which are his only birthright ! ' These passages show exactly the same nexus of emotion as we have analysed in Bunyan's use of the parable, and testify to the deep-rooted nature of the implications.

exist, while one brother gets the land (the source of production) and another gets only a mess of pottage (the low standard of living represented by wages).

In the next passage, from the *Fors Clavigera* of John Ruskin, this social consciousness of the Birthright has come full circle, for Ruskin is writing amid industrialized conditions where the means of actualizing Brotherhood are already visible. He begins by contrasting the ' common law of action ' by which trade-unionists bind themselves, with the rule of Capital which has kept workers in subjection and which capitalist ideologists have declared to be ' an eternal part of the Providential arrangements made for this world '. (Here we see the law of liberty and the imposed law put in contrast, not as hypotheses, but as organized actualities in final clash.) Ruskin goes on :

Trade Unions of England—Trade Armies of Christendom, what's the roll-call of you, and what part or lot have you, hitherto, in this Holy Christian Land of your Fathers?

Is not that heritage to be claimed, and the Birth Right of it, no less than the Death Right?

What talk you of wages? Whose is the wealth of the world but yours? Whose is the virtue? Do you mean to go on for ever, leaving your wealth to be consumed by the idle and your virtue to be mocked by the vile?

The wealth of the world is yours ; even your common rant and rabble of economists tell you that :—' no wealth without industry '. Who robs you of it, then, or beguiles you? Whose fault is it, you cloth-makers, that any English child is in rags? Whose fault is it, you shoemakers, that the street harlots mince in high-heeled shoes and your own babies paddle bare-foot in the street slime? Whose fault is it, you bronzed husbandman, that through all your furrowed England, children are dying of famine?

Here the abstraction of the Birthright is returned to the material facts of its genesis ; but the welding of idea and actuality now takes place on a higher level. The impasse that drove the concrete idea of Winstanley into the abstraction of Bunyan has been bridged ; the wound is healed, or in process of being healed. And note too how the doctrine of thrift reappears in new guise. No longer need the poor be virtuously thrifty, carrying the whole burden of productivity and ensuring that advance is continuous. They can now claim their Birthright.[1]

[1] It is noteworthy of the direct way that the age used the religious idiom for political purposes, that John Lilburne at his trial for high-treason in 1649 emphatically reiterated that he considered the bearing of Christ before Pilate as providing the model-basis for resistance to legal oppression. In his statement the words of Christ and the Petition of Right are inextricably blended. He says that he will not be trapped— ' I have learned more law out of the Petition of Right and Christ pleading before Pilate'. And when he is rebutting the charge that one of his books, dated May, can be made to come under treason-laws enacted in later months, he takes his stand on the apostolic : Where there is no law, there can be no transgression.

One more example of the Esau-parable. Francis Adams, in his *Songs of the Army of the Night*, addresses Imperialist England :

> Fond Esau, you who sold your high birthright
>   For gilded mud,
> Who did the wrong, and priest-like, called it right,
>   And swindled God !

10

Action at Last

S O Bunyan achieved the final wrench that left him
ecstatically helpless, and the emotion of election
and sustaining grace flowed in upon him in compensation. But this searching within for the conviction of grace had been accompanied by a search
without for a group among whom he could find his
needs echoed. The desire in Bunyan for concrete
activity, which had been up to this point the element
impeding his surrender, was still intact. The difference was that now it was no longer in opposition to
his inner life, as it had been except for the years in the
Army. Since the point of reconciliation had been
found, it could look outward, continually resolving
the conflict which, though persisting, had been robbed
of its sting. It found two forms of self-expression :
preaching and church-organization, and writing. The
success of Bunyan as a preacher and leader, the degree
of definitive form and objective perception that he
achieved in his writings, are the measure of the
resistances that had been formerly attached to the
Birthright-symbol.

One day he went tinkering into Bedford ; and in
one of the streets he came on three or four old women

sitting at a door in the sun, chatting of God with such serenity and certitude of spirit that he was fascinated. Here were those with whom he could join in fellowship. Without fellowship of some kind, without a group, however small, in which he could feel life being fashioned to the dictates of grace, so inherently active a person as Bunyan could never have stabilized his conversion. Indeed, he records that near the end of his inner conflict he felt himself ' inclining to a consumption ', and as spring came on, felt so weak that he thought he would die. He had reached the limits of his endurance. He would certainly have died unless he had found some means of liberating his energy outward.

Bedfordshire was on the whole strongly anti-prelatic, but in comparison with some other districts there seems to have been little violence adopted towards the royalist clergy, and the Elstow vicar, for instance, seems to have been left undisturbed, though mildly episcopalian. A Free Church had been started at Bedford in 1643 by a preacher who next year got into controversy at Coventry and was thrown into jail. In 1650 another and more stable attempt was made. This was the church that Bunyan joined. It was Independent, Congregationalist, with a Baptist tinge about it. Under Cromwell's tolerant Establishment it was presented with the parish church of St. John and its leader became the rector.

John Gifford was the leader, a not unremarkable man. An ardent royalist, he had in 1648 taken part in a rising in Kent. The royalists were defeated at Maidstone ; and Gifford with other officers was condemned to death. On the night before the executions, his sister visited him, found the sentinels drunk, and aided him to escape. He lay three days in a ditch, reached London, and finally took refuge at Bedford. There he practised as a physician ; but in his despair at the way things were going, he drank and gambled heavily. One night, after a loss of £15, in the midst of a violent rage, he picked up a book of devotions and a ' change of heart ' came over him : the need for something clean and positive. He frequented the meetings of the dissenters, and at last overcame their distrust. He was found a fervent preacher and assumed the leadership of the group. That his change of heart involved a new democratic emotion for him is shown by this charge in a letter written to his flock on his death-bed :

Let no respect of persons be in your comings-hither together. When you are met in Church there's neither rich nor poor, bond nor free, in Christ Jesus. 'Tis not a good practice to be offering places or seats when those who are rich come in . . .

He was an educated man, and the interest he took in Bunyan must have been valuable to the younger man. Bunyan by this time must have read a certain amount of doctrinal literature. Luther's *Commentary on the Galatians* had played an important part in bringing him to grace. But the guidance of Gifford must have contributed not a little to forming his mind.

He was formally received into the church at Bedford in 1653, after having been in touch with it for a year or two previously. He was the nineteenth person to join. He says that his attendance at Gifford's group caused such a village sensation that all the people of Elstow went along with him. They wanted to see what it was that had won over so notorious a sinner. It would seem, then, that his youthful reputation had been very bad indeed and took a great deal of living down. That his ' spiritual wrestlings ' had been indulged in with no attempts at privacy is shown by his remark in a book published in 1688 ; when ' God made him sigh ', he sighed with such stertorous agony that the neighbours would ask, ' What's the matter with John ? '

Two daughters were born to him. The first, Mary, was blind. She was born in July 1650 ; and the shock of her blindness may have had something to do in the final reduction of Bunyan to grace. In April 1654 another daughter was born ; and probably in 1655 he removed to Bedford. He had found a new life in the dissenting group and wished to partake of it with all the fullness possible. When Gifford dipped him under the waters of baptism, he had washed off all the past. It was Gifford, his father-in-God, to whom he now gave his loyalty ; and the old conflict, centring round his actual father Thomas, was resolved.

Bedford, a town of five parishes, but with much meadow and orchard within its bounds, had a population of between one and two thousand. Bunyan must have set up his workshop there ; and as we find him moving about the countryside preaching, he probably continued his itinerant tinkering, combining calling and vocation-in-God.

In 1655 Gifford died. There was a dispute over the

nomination of his successor. Some members of the Corporation tried to slip in their nominee ; but after protest the matter was referred to Cromwell, who decided in favour of John Burton, a pious, informed, but sickly youth. About this time Bunyan seems first to have been drawn to ' discover his gift among them '. His preaching was most successful ; and people came ' by hundreds, and that from all parts, though ', he adds with a touch of satire, ' under sundry and diverse accounts '. He did not relish being taken as a rare monster, an eloquent tinker.

After preaching about a year he came into energetic conflict with the Quakers, whose doctrine of universal grace upset all Bunyan's painfully-constructed conviction of Election. But more on that subject later. The interest here of his battle with the Quakers is that he was led into writing a polemic, and then a reply to the Quaker reply. The inarticulate, stupefied tinker was now an author.

In 1657 he was nominated for trial as a deacon with three others. But he was not selected, as it was considered that Brother Bunyan was ' taken off by preaching of the Gospel '. The congregation did not wish to encroach on his preaching activities. He was an important person. The brooding, indrawn tinker was now a preacher filled with fire, tireless.

11

Preaching Tinker

IN March 1658 he was in some trouble at Eaton, the result of zealous preaching ; but nothing seems to have come of it. We also hear of him in conflict with ministers of more orthodox opinions. In May 1659 he was preaching in a barn at Toft in Cambridgeshire, by special invitation ; and one Thomas Smith of Cambridge, once a rector of Gawcat, professor of Arabic, attacked him after the service for uncharitableness in telling the congregation he knew most of them to be unbelievers. As a warrant, Bunyan cited Christ's parable of the four seeds, only one of which took root. The discussion ended with Smith denying that Bunyan had any right to preach. Bunyan was not ordained, and the lay congregation at Bedford could not invest him with any rights.

A few weeks later Smith published a letter on the subject of the debate, emphasizing Bunyan's social status. 'A wandering preaching tinker. . . . Your tinker.' Bunyan did not reply, but another Cambridge man took up his defence in a pamphlet. ' You seem to be angry with the tinker because he strives to mend souls as well as kettles and pans. . . .'

Another invitation to preach, of which we know,

came from William Dell, rector of Yelden. Dell was a sturdy fighter for the right to freedom of expression ; he had been chaplain to the Army under Fairfax ; and he wished to disestablish the Church in every shape and form. ' In nature ', he said, ' is no external uniformity ; variety of form in the world is the beauty of the world '. In giving Bunyan his pulpit, and on a Christmas day too, he scandalized the well-to-do of the neighbourhood ; and they remembered it against him, and brought it up at once in a petition to have him ejected, as soon as the Restoration occurred. He had declared ' in the public congregation that he had rather hear a plain countryman speak in the church that came from the plough than the best orthodox minister that was in the country '. And Bunyan is cited as ' one Bunyan, of Bedford, a tinker '.

The insistence of the masses on their right to think and preach their own religion was an essential part of the revolutionary movement. For such a claim undermined the whole ideology of absolutism. Nothing astonished and outraged the reactionaries so much as the spectacle of a working-man in the pulpit. John Walker, who compiled a huge book on the sufferings of the orthodox clergy during the Rebellion and Commonwealth, never loses a chance to mention the appearance of a weaver, tapster, pedlar, mason, or such, as a preacher. The vast changes that went on over England can be better felt by a reading of Walker's four-hundred-page folio, double-column small type, than by a consideration of the purely political innovations. Again and again we find comments such as the following about Chelmsford : he has been recounting the riots and dissentings, and ends, ' Nor could it be otherwise expected, when by that time the Town was governed by a Tinker, two Cobblers, two Tailors, two Pedlars, etc.'

When we read passages such as this, ' by Education a Weaver, of no University, yet one that hath a Charge of souls in Nottinghamshire ', we understand why Bunyan was so touchy on the question of education. Walker several times mentions tinkers as preachers ; and elsewhere one hears of a preacher in Herts., Rice the Tinker of Aston (whose fellows were a bodice-maker, a tailor, and a collar-maker).

The following passages from Walker, chosen at random, will give some idea of the wrath and pertur-bation caused among the upper classes by the advent of mechanics as the accepted prophets of the people :

> Vile, undeserving, poor curates, poor schoolmasters, poor lecturers, poor vicars, poor New Lights, were substituted in their places ; hardly one that had been a Fellow of a College, or had been at any time in the University ; but poor scholars, servitors, and curates. (*Cumberland.*)

> He had formerly been a Skinner or Glover ; but now being a man of more than common Merit in the Gospel, that he might not be put upon the Temptation of taking up his old trade, and Skinning instead of Fleecing his Flock, he had the benefice doubled to him. (*Shropshire.*)

> One . . . who was the Hog-herd's son of Little-Houghton, had been bred a knitter, became afterwards a horse-buyer, but then Mayor of Northampton, Colonel of the Town-Regiment, and as it seems, at that time also the Ordinary of the place—ordered that, when they came to inter the skin and bones of this starved Martyr (for flesh

he had none, as the *Mercury* observes) that no other form should be used, than this :

Ashes to Ashes, Dust to Dust ;
Here's the Pit, and in you must. (*Wellingborough.*)

If a cobbler or a tinker get into the pulpit and preach four or five hours for the Parliament, these are the men nowadays. (*Suffolk.*)

They did put out good ministers and put in pedlars, tinkers, and cobblers. (*Isle of Ely.*)

Wat Tyler—I mean Wat Long, whom some call Col. Long—came with some troops of horse and cast his whole family out. (*I.e. the royalist rector's family.*) (*Rayne, Essex.*)

Soon after his vicarage was supplied successively by a weaver and two plowmen. (*Herts.*)

He had declaimed against the Authority of Parliaments, and affirmed that the Parliament-men are Mechanics and Illiterate, and had nothing to do to intermeddle in matters of religion. (*Chigwell, Bucks.*)

These passages give us some idea of the social upheaval that was going on, and the fear with which it afflicted the masters. ' The seditious pamphlets, the tumultuous risings of rude multitudes threatening blood and destruction, the preaching of cobblers, feltmakers, tailors, grooms, and women ', thus a writer of 1642 summed up the results of Anabaptism.

When the people broke into the churches and smashed the rails round the communion-tables, or dragged the communion-table away from its altar arrangement and put it in the middle of the church like any ordinary table in a room, or assaulted the minister who wore a surplice, and so on, they were not ' fanatics ' : they were expressing their emotion of common brotherhood. They were all brothers and sisters in Christ. Why, then, rail the table off and magic it into a thing apart ? Why isolate the minister as a person apart, the hieratic emblem of class domination ? If they were going to partake of the ' divine body ', they meant to do it in the homely fashion of their customary meals. They wanted to smash the web of magic, to end the fixed and authorized services which expressed the rigid class-laws putting them in their places. They didn't want ritual : they wanted preachers who were men out of their ranks, men who could expound things understandably, profitably, as an aid in daily life.

Thwarted of socially-constructive self-expression, they devised their churches as compensations. The bourgeois, who still wanted strict form and control, built up the Presbyterian form, an excellent system of committees knitted together ; the lower classes turned more towards Independency, the local free church feeling itself in communion with its brother-churches everywhere, but not linked up. These two forms together comprised the whole skeletal machinery for a complete democracy ; for their methods of delegation, their committee-forms, were premonitions, not of parliamentary government, but of the secular forms of freedom emerging in trade-unions, in co-operative societies, and in the Paris Commune and the Russian Soviets. They were, so to speak, constructions *outside society* of what the people felt that society lacked and must continue to lack while organized on a class-basis.

It was in this atmosphere of democratic activity

that Bunyan wrote his third book, *A Few Sighs from Hell*. It is lurid with hell-terror—and that is the expression of the sense of dissatisfaction and instability, of ceaseless crisis, resulting from the fact that the democratization was based on an outside-society formulation, not on a concrete social order. But it is also a healthy warning to the wealthy classes, the cause of the instability. It is built on the parable of Lazarus and Dives, the poor man who goes to heaven and the heartless rich man who goes to hell. For if the upper classes were watching, with fear masked as scorn, the irruption of mechanics into places reserved for their betters, the lower classes were retorting distrust for distrust.

For instance, Mrs. Hutchinson wrote of her husband, who, though a stout anti-prelate, was at heart a landed country-gentleman :

He had experience not only of the ungodly and ill-affected, but even of the godly themselves, who thought it scarcely possible for anyone to continue a gentleman, and firm to a godly interest, and therefore repaid all his vigilancy and labours for them with a very unjust jealousy.

Bunyan repudiates wealth in this book of his on damned Dives.

I tell thee, friend, there are some promises that the Lord hath helped me to lay hold of Jesus Christ through and by, that I would not have out of the Bible for as much gold as can lie between York and London, piled up to the stars.

But to deal with this, we had better take a new chapter.

12

The Gift of Grace

DURING these years, as Bunyan himself tells us, he was in a tearing rage against sin, breathing hell-fire on his listeners. His book about the damned rich, based on a sermon, is clearly the kind of thing he was preaching ; and this type of denunciation of the lordly and the rich was exactly in key with the democratic agitation, speaking through religious terms, which the passages by Walker describe.

Yet, by the contradiction we have analysed in the notion of grace, Bunyan was working out rigidly his idea of predestination and election at the same time as he was shouting that Dives was damned. That is, he was helping to create the ideology of capitalism while personally uttering his detestation of the capitalist.

It was not gold he wanted. He spoke the truth in saying that. But he wanted to reconcile himself with the world and at the same time to feel that he was building on his sense of human unity. There is a passage in *Grace Abounding* which expresses perfectly the dilemma of the man who wants security, yet realizes that only the human bond, not possessions, can make him feel secure :

JOHN BUNYAN

It was glorious to me to see his (Christ's) exaltation, and the worth and prevalency of all his benefits, and that because of this : now I could look from myself to him, and should reckon that all those graces of God that now were green in me, were yet but like those cracked groats and fourpence-halfpennies that rich men carry in their purses, when their gold is in their trunks at home. O, I saw my gold was in my trunk at home. In Christ, my Lord and Saviour. Now Christ was all.

Wealth is the symbol of social security. Bunyan is driven to use the symbol of gold to express his sense of Christ's value. Yet in a class-rent society, that which makes secure also makes insecure. So, he that has been driven to seek for reality finds nothing steadfast in wealth ; he feels only the bond which is being created out of the methods of producing wealth. But, being unaware of this dynamic relation between the thing he scorns and the emotion he desires, he is forced to abstract the latter and symbolize it in the body of redeeming unity. Yet an unconscious sense of the relation obtrudes ; and that is why Bunyan, like so many Christians before him and after, is forced to think of his redemption-symbol as a nice deposit in heaven, gold in the bank of the Father, a treasure above. It *is* wealth he wants : for what is wealth but a sign of the human power to join together and master nature ? Yet wealth as it actually exists in his world, being the property of a master-class, is the enemy. Since wealth destroys the harmony of human relationships, he feels compelled to choose between Christ and money—wealth as co-operative activity, and wealth as a class-weapon.

THE GIFT OF GRACE

Another passage which brings out clearly the relation of wealth and grace is the following speech by Hopeful in *The Pilgrim's Progress* :

' When you shall have done all those things that are commanded you, say : We are unprofitable.' . . . From whence (such texts as this) I began to reason with myself thus : If all my righteousnesses are filthy rags, if by the deeds of the law no man can be justified, and if, when we have done all, we are yet unprofitable, then it is but folly to think of heaven by the Law.

I further thought thus : If a man runs a hundred pounds into the shopkeeper's debt, and, after that, shall pay for all that he shall fetch ; yet his old debt stands still in the book uncrossed ; for the which the shopkeeper may sue him, and cast him into prison till he shall pay the debt.

That is, the rule of the Law is the oppressive system, masked by the money-symbol, in which man preys on man, and the ' debt ' is the emblem of pressure and insecurity. Grace wipes out the debt and gives a new start. But it is not merely a new start on the old level. Hence the fierce insistence of the Calvinist that the man who was once redeemed cannot fall back into sin, into the world ruled by the Law.

But how can the old debt, the burden of the Old Man, be wiped out in such a way that relapse is utterly impossible ? Clearly, only if the money-symbol ceases to be the oppressive mask of the Law, the screen behind which man preys on man. But to wipe out the debt by raising the whole human basis to a level where debts on the old system cannot be incurred, where the new start means a start that cannot by any means bring a man back to the old servitude of debt, there must be some communist organization whereby production for use is established. That, however, is historically impossible in Bunyan's day. Therefore, the desire for escape from the body of this death, the Law, is abstracted into the notion of Redemption.

We may note that this notion of the absolute incompatibility of Grace and the Law is basic in all Bunyan's thought. When the Son of Redemption faces Diabolus, the Father of Slavery, in *The Holy War*, Diabolus offers to surrender and rule Mansoul according to the Law. His offer is scornfully rejected as the limit of evil.

In a passage in one of his last books Bunyan shows clearly his sense of class divisions ; but he is a tired man, lacking the indignation that thirty years before urged him to dwell on the picture of the rich man in hell :

The difference between us and them is, not that we are really two, but one body in Christ, in divers places. True we are below stairs and they above ; they in their holiday and we in our working-day clothes ; they in harbour, but we in the storm ; they at rest, and we in the wilderness ; they singing as crowned with joy, we crying as crowned with thorns. But I say, we are all of one house, one family, and are all children of one Father.

It was the inevitable conclusion of the attempt at reconciliation he had made : an attempt which was at root a wish to accept historical process. The poor were indeed, for the time being, doomed to drudgery. But the abstract effort to accept process ends in picturing this state of things as an eternal law.

THE GIFT OF GRACE

That picture, however, lay at the end of the road, long after the King had come back. Under the Commonwealth Bunyan did not feel so ready to accept class divisions. In 1659, he followed up the enjoyed picture of the rich man sweltering in the manifold and detailed horrors of hell with *The Doctrine of the Law and Grace Unfolded*. Here he makes a passionate attack on the ' Law '. The life in Christ is life ' under grace '.

Like all other Protestants, he becomes entangled, in his exposition, in all the logical inconsistencies which follow from trying to state that the redeemed-in-Christ utterly reject the Law, and yet live the good life out of the richness of their communion with Christ, their unfailing and unerring gift of grace.

Behind these arguments there lurk the same complexities of contradiction as we saw in the use made of the term Nature. The tyrannical Law of good works is an abstraction from the constituted equity laws of class-society. These have to be obeyed ; yet they are for ever in conflict with the deepening sense of the human bond. It is that sense which is the only thing worth having in the world ; yet how are we to relate it to a world that denies and insults it ?

It was the degrees in which this dilemma was felt that made the divergences in the Protestant churches. Each section arrested the problem of grace at a different point of relation to the Law, according to the ease or otherwise with which they were able to come to terms with the world. Only the Quakers went to the extreme of utterly repudiating the Law, announcing a universal free grace, and considering that a man should always follow his impulse. (There were, of course, many other sects who had similar ideas ; but the Quakers survived out of the welter to become an influential body.) The tendencies of anarchism in this creed were demonstrated when James Nayler allowed himself to be browbeaten by a woman admirer who had simply made up her mind that he *must* be Jesus ; he let her and a few more adherents lead him into Bristol with cries of ' Holy, holy ', and was brutally punished for it (Mr. Downing, M.P., making the historic remark, ' Our God is here supplanted—O horrid ! ').

Bunyan, with his practical sense, had felt this spirit of wild anarchism that animated the early Quakers ; and it was on account of it that he had attacked them. For all his anxieties, he never lost his streak of practicality ; he went on working as a tinker. George Fox threw up work altogether and wandered round with his visions and his blazing eyes and his piercing rhetoric, starving or eating what he was given. Fox never had the lengthy period of tormented self-analysis that Bunyan had known. The result was that when Bunyan constructed his system of grace, he devised an ideology closely related to the social processes in which he and his class, the dispossessed peasantry on the edge of the petty-bourgeois, were involved.

But always there remained with him a strong sense of hatred of the Law. He never lost his sense that the life of grace was threatened by the Law—that the struggle for unity was denied by the existing society. Even in the passage given above, in which he carries his reconciliation as far as it will go, the strong terms in which he draws the diverging class-fates show a sense of injustice which breaks the pact it is trying to strike. And in his great allegories, though dealing with the life of the individual, the urgency of the sense of struggle carries with it deeper implications. Especially is *The Pilgrim's Progress* a protest of the struggling individual against the Law. Christian opposes to the Law the heroism of the man who lives 'under grace', who cares only for the love which is unity. But we shall deal with that aspect when the time comes.

These schisms within the Christian Church are interestingly paralleled by the Chassidic revolt within the Judaic faith. Chassidism was a revolt of the Jewish masses against the Talmudic and Rabbinic aristocracy who taught that study of the 'Law' could alone lead to God. The Chassidic dissenters asserted, as against the rule of the Law, the creed that by joyous fulfilment of the simple daily commandments and the interpretations of their Rebbes, they could win equally to the Father's favour. Later the Chassidic leaders lost their fervour and, like the late Methodist preachers, found ways of coming to terms with the world.

13

Persecution

SOMETIME in 1659 Bunyan's wife died. If he was not quite so hasty as his father had been in re-marriage, he did not lose much time in finding another wife. There were four young children—two boys as well as the girls—to be looked after : a task which Bunyan, with his preaching and his church duties, in addition to his daily labour, could hardly be expected to meet adequately on his own.

The diversity of theme in the discussions at the church is illustrated by an entry of April 1660 : 'The 16th day of the next month to be spent in seeking God with reference to the affairs of the nation, and the weakness of our brother Burton'.

But this pleasant state of things, in which the little congregation could feel themselves equally called upon to deal with national politics and the morals of the next-door neighbour, was not to last much longer. How little the progressive sections of Bedfordshire realized the landslide that was shortly to occur, is shown by a Petition sent to Parliament in June 1659. 'Divers freeholders and others' asked for the removal of Tithes, the reformation of the Courts of Law, the establishment of Religious Toleration, the safeguarding of the citizen against imprisonment or distraint except for a legally-defined crime. More important, they asked that the militia be put under the command of men faithful to the good old cause ; otherwise there was no efficient defence against reaction.

When the Convention Parliament was called next year, two of the four Bedfordshire members were royalist. The middle class had turned against the Republic. The restoration of the King was assured.

Charles II had promised Toleration ; but that was the last thing the bourgeoisie wanted. Even what backing the Presbyterians had had now rapidly fell away ; and there were left only the Episcopalians and the lower-class dissenting groups as significant forces.

To Bunyan belongs the honour of having led the vanguard of sufferers for liberty. On 12 November 1660, the Justices at Bedford passed the order for the restoring of the Book of Common Prayer in the churches of the county ; but as yet there was no legal prohibition against the dissenters. Therefore the action that was taken against Bunyan was entirely illegal ; but its illegality did not prevent it from succeeding.

About a month after the Order was passed, Bunyan went to address a meeting at the hamlet of Lower Samsell, by Harlington, some thirteen miles south of Bedford. The service was to be held in a farmhouse surrounded by elms except on the side looking to the Barton Hills ; a moated farm-house, like so many in lonely districts, with a drawbridge that could be lifted at night. There was a hawthorn in the field, in the shade of which, tradition said, Bunyan had often preached. But this was in November, and the service was to be within the house.

Rumours had spread that Francis Wingate, the neighbouring magistrate, had issued a warrant for Bunyan's arrest ; and the farmer raised the question whether the service should be held. ' I think ', says Bunyan, ' he was more afraid for me than for himself '. Bunyan refused to consider abandoning the service. (Was not the Book of Common Prayer ' pottage ' ? the symbol of bondage to feudalism and to greed ?)

No, Bunyan could not submit to the world which had set up the Book of Common Prayer, the mess of pottage, as the supreme value. He answered the timid brethren :

No, by no means ; I will not stir, neither will I have the meeting dismissed for this. Come, be of good cheer, let us not be daunted. Our cause is good, we need not be ashamed of it ; to preach God's word is so good a work that we shall be well rewarded even if we suffer for it.

As there was yet some time before the service began, Bunyan went out of the house and walked up and down in the field, beside the bare elms. It was a moment of winter. He must face the enemy full in the eyes ; he must be ready to strip himself of all the comfort and bravery of summer hopes ; he must be ready to stand stark, naked to the bone of resistance, amid the lashing winds. He had no doubts, but it was a bitter moment. If he were to fail, he thought, what a blow it would be to the cause ; what a discouragement to all the new converts and the weaker hearts who looked to him for leadership. If he were the man picked out to lead the forlorn hope in a world that knew not unity, it was his honour. If he failed, the gospel of grace would be stained.

Serene, confirmed, he went back into the house. His friends had gathered, the men and women who shared with him the precious meal of fellowship. Along elm-ways and over the fields they had gathered from many hamlets ; and with resolute voice he spoke the opening prayer. The prayer was said, and the leaves of the Bibles were turned, and Bunyan lifted up his voice and heart. The answering voice came ; the voice of the Law. The constable had appeared, with Wingate's man, and he bade Bunyan stop the service and go along with them. Bunyan told his brethren not to be depressed, for it was a mercy to suffer in a good cause. They might, he said, have been arrested for theft or murder, but blessed be God, it was not so ; they were only Christians suffering for the right ; and after all it was better to be persecuted than to persecute. So they went out.

Magistrate Wingate was from home. A friend— doubtless a farmer known to the officers—engaged to look after the prisoner and produce him next morning. ' Otherwise ', says Bunyan, ' constable must have charged a watch with me, or have secured me some other ways, my crime was so great '.

Next morning they went to the constable, and then on to the J.P. Wingate had now returned. His house lay near Harlington Church, in an angle of cross-roads. Passing the church, the party went through the heavy gateway and entered the hall, probably facing Wingate in the main parlour, a low-ceilinged room with panelled walls and oaken crossbeams with a carved rose-boss for centre. Wingate was about the same age as Bunyan—in the early thirties —though the vicar's daughter whom he had married had already borne him nine children. He seems to have been a haughty, not very intelligent man ; and he was keen to do his class-duty and crush the pestilent tinker, law or no law.

They stood face to face : the country squire who had been a royalist refugee at Oxford in the early years of the Civil War and whose mother had had her jointure-estate sequestered and had paid a fine of £100 to the Parliament ; and the preaching tinker whose sole property was the Birthright he had refused to sell. And now we remember the self-assured master only because he took on himself the rôle of persecuting the tinker.

Wingate fell back on an old statute of 35 Elizabeth to excuse his persecution of Bunyan ; but as yet there was no law enacted against dissent by Charles II, while on the other hand there was the Declaration of Breda, promising liberty and consideration for tender consciences, which should have protected Bunyan, if the King meant to act honourably.

Wingate asked the constable questions about the behaviour of the meeting where Bunyan had been arrested. He hoped to get some evidence which would enable him to charge the meeting with seditious intent, with plots of armed revolt. The meeting, however, was so obviously peaceable that he had to abandon this trick. He turned roughly to Bunyan and asked him what he meant by his behaviour ; why he wasn't content with following his calling. For it was against the law, he said, that such men as Bunyan should act as he had.

Bunyan replied that he came only to instruct and counsel those who required his aid, and that there was no reason why his work at the forge should interfere with his preaching. Wingate retorted angrily that he would break the neck of such meetings. Bunyan answered with dignity, ' It may be so '.

Sureties were called. They were ready. Wingate warned the men who gave their bond that unless they kept Bunyan from preaching they would lose their money. Bunyan at once released them from their undertaking. Nothing, he said, would stop him from speaking of God's Word. Wingate, pleased, said that Bunyan would have to go to jail ; and he went into another room to draw up the mittimus.

While he was thus absent, in came the vicar of Harlington, 'an old enemy of the truth, Dr. Lindall'. Lindall taunted and reviled Bunyan. Bunyan said that he had not come thither to talk with him, but with the magistrate. Lindall took this rebuke to mean that Bunyan had been silenced ; so he went on with his insults, jeering and asking why Bunyan had ' meddled with that for which he could show no

warrant '. Had he taken the oaths ? If not, jail
was the place for him.

Bunyan told him that he would answer any sober
questions. Lindall confidently asked him to prove
his right to preach. Bunyan quoted Peter, ' As
every man hath received the gift, even so let him
minister the same '.

Lindall said, ' Aye, to whom is that spoken ? '

' To whom ? Why, to every man that hath re-
ceived a gift from God. Mark, saith the Apostle,
" As every man that hath received a gift from God ".
And again, " You may prophesy one by one ".'

Lindall was somewhat abashed, but answered sar-
castically, ' Indeed I do remember that I have read
of one Alexander, a coppersmith, who did much
oppose and disturb the apostles '.

Aiming, it is like, at me (comments Bunyan),
because I was a tinker.

Bunyan replied that he had also read of very many
priests and pharisees that had their hands in the blood
of our Lord Jesus Christ.

Lindall had no retort left now except abuse. He
said, ' Aye, and you are one of those scribes and
pharisees ; for you, with a pretence, make long
prayers to devour widows' houses '.

Bunyan replied that if Lindall had got no more than
he, Bunyan, had by preaching and praying, then
Lindall would not be so rich as he now was. Then,
recalling the Scripture : ' Answer not a fool according to his folly ', he gave up trying to make debating-
points and said no more than was necessary to make
Lindall see that he was not overbearing him.

PERSECUTION

This debate brings out strongly the two irreconcilable class-positions, each able to base itself with an equal show of logic on the Scriptures. Bunyan could quote texts absolutely vindicating his reliance on grace ; the Episcopalian could build up an equally effective case for absolute submission to the constituted authorities. The conclusions depended on the point of departure ; and that point lay in class-needs. We see how the upper and middle-class Protestants, now that the second stage of the Protestant revolution was reached, abhorred the arguments which their fathers had used in the attack on feudal authority. The continued pressure of dissent, with its resistance to the State as the ally of the State-Church and to the State-Church as the ally of vested interests, was an essential part of the movement into democracy.

Wingate had now made out the mittimus, and Bunyan set out for Bedford Jail with the constable. Going down the hill, they met two friends of Bunyan's, who thought that something might yet be done. So Bunyan and the constable waited while these friends made an attempt to wean Wingate from his severity. After a while the men came back with the message that if Bunyan would say certain words to Wingate, he might be released. Bunyan answered that if the words were such as could be spoken with a good conscience, he would say them ; not otherwise.

They all went back to the house. The November dusk was drawing on, and while they were waiting in one of the rooms, in came from another room

JOHN BUNYAN

William Foster, later Dr. Foster, a Bedford lawyer, a crawling bully. He had married Wingate's sister seven years before, but had now been a widower for a year. He came into the room with a candle in his hand ; and seeing Bunyan, he lifted up the candle, cried, ' What, John Bunyan ! ' and made as if to embrace him. Bunyan drew back, wondering why so well known an opposer of dissent should now fawn with smiles on him. Foster began arguing with oily persuasiveness, trying to get Bunyan to promise to give up preaching.

Again there was a debate on the right of a man who did not possess the authorization of Bishop and Parliament to preach. Foster appealed to the law, Bunyan to the impulse of grace. Foster said that Bunyan neglected his calling to preach ; that his hearers were nothing but ' a company of poor, simple, ignorant people '. Bunyan replied that he durst not betray the work to which he had been called.

At last Foster went out, and several of Wingate's servants began to argue with Bunyan, saying that he stood on a mere nicety and that if he would promise not to preach he would be immediately released. Bunyan stood steadfast. Then both Wingate and Foster came in and talked at him, but he still stood steadfast. As he left the house, he felt the deep ' peace of God ', the peace of integrated conviction, fill his being.

It was late. So he was kept in custody till next morning, and then went off to Bedford Jail, along the miry roads.

PERSECUTION

The brethren had now all heard of Bunyan's arrest, and an effort was made to enlist Mr. Crompton, J.P., of Elstow. Crompton seems to have been friendlily disposed ; but the sheer illegality of the charge against Bunyan made him think that there was something deeper in the whole business, some touch of sedition, and so he feared to intervene.

14

Trial

BUNYAN lay in prison seven or eight weeks awaiting the January Quarter Sessions. The Sessions and Assizes were held in an old building called the Chapel of Herne, which was usually leased to one of the townsfolk with a clause compelling him to vacate and leave it cleared when courts were to be held. Here Bunyan appeared in the second week of January 1661. There were five magistrates on the bench. The chairman, Sir John Kelynge, was a cowardly bully of the Foster type ; he once fined a jury 100 marks apiece for acquitting some poor people charged with meeting for worship with Bibles but no Prayer Books. Another of the magistrates was Wingate's uncle ; a third had just been knighted by the King ; a fourth was knighted shortly after. This last man, Sir George Blundell, had had his estate decimated by the Commonwealth and he was now eager to persecute. We find him still in 1670 harrying Quakers and other dissenters ; once when no one would bid for distrained property, he swore that he would sell a cow for a shilling rather than that the work should not go forward.

Before this bench of royalists John Bunyan, of the

town of Bedford, labourer, was indicted for ' devilishly
and perniciously abstaining from coming to church
to hear divine service, and for being a common upholder of several unlawful meetings and conventicles,
to the great disturbance and distraction of the good
subjects of this kingdom, contrary to the laws of our
sovereign Lord the King '.

The clerk of the Court asked him what he had to
say to the charge. Bunyan replied that he did indeed
go to the church of God, and was by grace a member
of the people over whom Christ is the Head.
Kelynge at once interrupted, ' Do you come to
church—you know what I mean ; to parish church,
to hear divine service ? '

' No ', said Bunyan, ' I do not '.

The old debate began all over again : the Church
as an instrument of class oppression, as a sanctifying
reflection of the State ; the Church as a grouping
of men and women obeying the impulse of unity as
far as the pressure of historical limitations would
permit.

Kelynge, with ruling-class insolence, tried to bear
down the subtle tinker, but came the worse off
from the encounter. To him prayer must be
institutional, to buttress the State forms. To Bunyan prayer had to be a free outpouring of emotion,
a communion of grace. One of the bench tried to
stop Bunyan speaking, considering that an insult to
the Book of Common Prayer was blasphemy. Kelynge
said, ' No, no, never fear him. We are better established than so. He can do no harm '. And added
the astonishingly illiterate comment, ' We know the

Common Prayer Book hath been ever since the apostles' time, and is lawful for it to be used in the Church '.

The argument went on. The bench told Bunyan that he was possessed by a devil, and that his god was Beelzebub. When he spoke of the 'comfortable presence of God' at the meetings, and added, 'For ever blessed be His holy name', Kelynge sneered, saying that he talked Pedlar's French, and bade him leave off canting.

Next began the familiar argument on the right of an unordained tinker to preach. Kelynge tried to be crushingly facetious. 'Let me', he said, 'a little open that Scripture to you. As every man hath received the gift—that is, as every man hath received a trade—so let him follow it. If any man have received a gift of tinkering, as thou hast done, let him follow his tinkering ; and so other men their trades and the preacher his '.

(This crude interpretation of Kelynge's was not without historical warrant. For what do we see as the tendency during the years when Christianity was conquering in the Roman world ? We see just this kind of ossification into castes which became the social forms of medieval life. Under medievalism most men acquiesced in the Church's teachings, because in a static community they did indeed feel that a man's calling in work was his vocation in God. Kelynge, as the feudalist, champions this attitude. Bunyan, as the spokesman of the class that was building the future, that used the idiom of grace-inspiration to express their sense of movement out of orthodox and static forms, championed the dynamic side of the apostolic teachings. In a caste-system such as the Hindu, we may note, calling and vocation are absolutely inseparable ; and it is religion which rivets the iron bond of each caste.)

Bunyan retorted to Kelynge by showing that the next verse of the scriptural passage in question referred definitely to the ' oracles of God '. Kelynge, out-argued, soon closed the debate and declared that the court could not wait on Bunyan any longer. He demanded to know if Bunyan confessed the indictment.

Now for the first time, Bunyan says, he knew that he was being indicted. He answered that he and his brethren had their meetings of sweet comfort and encouragement. To that he pleaded guilty, but to nothing else.

Kelynge, with no more ado, sentenced Bunyan to three months' imprisonment. If he thereafter preached, he was to be banished from England. If he returned from banishment without the King's permission, he would be hanged.

As the jailer was taking him off, Bunyan said to the bench : ' I am at a point with you. For if I were out of prison to-day, I would preach the Gospel again to-morrow, by the help of God.'

One of the magistrates said something ; but Bunyan did not hear what it was, as the jailer was pulling him away.

During the three months of his sentence he was visited by Cobb, the clerk of the peace. The magistrates wanted to extort from him a promise

of submission to the constituted Church authorities.
If he failed to submit, Cobb told him, he would be
hardly treated at the next sessions ; he would
probably be banished, or suffer even worse things.
Cobb based his appeal on the fact of Venner's
Insurrection in London ; a group of Fifth Monarchy
men who considered it impious to accept any earthly
king had rebelled. Bunyan denied the relevance of
the comparison between himself and Venner. Cobb
insisted that meetings of dissenters could not be
tolerated, as they hatched sedition. He seems to
have been an amiable man who was merely carrying
out instructions ; and he showed a strange sense of
geography in warning Bunyan that he might be
transported to such fearsome places as Spain or
Constantinople. Bunyan answered that he stood
to the truth to the last drop of his blood, and
quoted Wiclif in his support.

Cobb could only fall back on the statement that
as the King was ordained of God and had forbidden
meetings, ' therefore you should not have any '.

Bunyan served out his full sentence of three
months, and should have then been released. But
as a dissenting preacher was not a person who
could claim the protection of something that so
much belonged to his masters as the Law, he was
simply kept in jail, illegally, for a further six years.
He says himself how his ignorance of the law worried
him, for he did not know on what to base his legal
stand or what his persecutors could legally threaten.
It is important to realize all these strands of fear
and hostility, this sense of being excluded as an

alien, when we seek to evaluate the content of Bunyan's hatred of the ' Law '.

In August was held the Midsummer Assize. Bunyan hoped to gain a hearing in open court. He must have felt that anything was better than the anxiety of waiting on an unformulated menace. But his persecutors knew better than to let him into court again. His wife, Elizabeth, fought loyally on his behalf. Three times she presented petitions to the Judge of Assize, begging that her husband's case should be tried.

She went up to London and spoke with Lord Barkwood, giving him a petition. He and some other Lords who read the petition said that they had no power to release Bunyan, but had committed his release to the judges at the next Assize. When the Assize came, she approached the kindly Sir Matthew Hale. He told her that he would do what he could, but feared it would be little. Next day in St. Paul's Square she threw a petition into the window of a carriage in which the other judge, Twisden, was riding, on his way from the Swan Inn to the court-room. Twisden snapped at her and said that Bunyan would not be let out till he abjured preaching.

She decided to have another try at Hale. She managed to get into the court, make her way through the throng, and step up before the bench during some pause. Hale again spoke encouragingly, but one of the justices who had condemned Bunyan, Wingate's uncle, stated that Bunyan had been legally convicted and that he was a hot-blooded fellow who deserved what he had got.

Undeterred, she went to the Swan Chamber, where the judges, with several magistrates and gentry of the county, were met. With abashed face and trembling heart, she held to her purpose. She made her plea, addressing Hale. He answered again kindly, but said he could do nothing. She pointed out the entire illegality of the proceedings. ' My lord, he is kept unlawfully in prison ; they clapped him up before there was any proclamation against the meetings ; the indictment also is false. Besides, they never asked him whether he was guilty or no ; neither did he confess the indictment '.

A magistrate considered it sufficient refutation of her argument to declare that the conviction was lawful. She argued on. Twisden grew rude and angry. Chester, Wingate's uncle, kept on reiterating, ' It is recorded, woman, it is recorded '. (As if, says Bunyan, it must be true if it was recorded.) Mrs. Bunyan told of her visit to London and the promise made by the Lords to commit Bunyan's release to the judges of the next Assize. The judges conveniently became deaf when she started on this subject, leaving Chester to repeat, ' It is recorded ', or ' He is convicted '. When she turned on him and said that if the records had it so, then the records were false, he became vituperative, called Bunyan a pestilent fellow, and said he had no like in the whole county. Twisden at last announced that Bunyan could go free if he promised not to preach, for as a preacher he was a breaker of the peace.

Mrs. Bunyan said that her husband desired to live peaceably and to follow his calling, that his family might be maintained. 'My lord', she said, 'I have four small children that cannot help themselves, of which one is blind, and have nothing to live upon but the charity of good people'.

Hale was interested. (Mrs. Bunyan must have been in her teens; for since very early marriages were common, he would otherwise not have been so astonished at her having four children. Wingate, for instance, had married his Lettice when she was fifteen.) 'Hast thou four children?' he asked. 'Thou art but a young woman to have four children.'

'My lord', she answered, 'I am but mother-in-law to them, having not been married to him yet full two years. Indeed I was with child when my husband was first apprehended; but being young, and unaccustomed to such things, I being smayed at the news, fell into labour, and so continued for eight days, and then was delivered, but my child died.'

Hale said, 'Poor woman'.

But Twisden snarled out that she made poverty her cloak and that Bunyan had made a better thing out of his runabout preaching than out of tinker's work.

'What is his calling?' asked Hale.

'A tinker, my lord', said several of the company, with a ready sneer.

Mrs. Bunyan looked at them. 'Yes', she said, 'and because he is a tinker, and a poor man, therefore he is despised, and cannot have justice'.

Hale, in his gentlest voice, said, 'I tell thee, woman, seeing it is so, that they have taken what thy husband spake for a conviction, thou must either apply thyself to the King, or sue out his pardon, or get a writ of error '.

Chester was enraged at the suggestion a writ of error could be taken out. He burst out once more against Bunyan. Mrs. Bunyan stoutly defended her husband as one who had done much good. Twisden joined in, growing so infuriated that he seemed about to strike her, and swearing that Bunyan's doctrine was of the devil. Mrs. Bunyan retorted sharply that some day a ' righteous Judge ' would decide about that—and presumably also about unrighteous judges who oppressed the poor. Twisden, irritated beyond measure, turned to Hale and said, ' Do not mind her, but send her away '.

Hale once more, in a friendly voice, gave her the only advice that he could give. Chester, in fury, pulled off his hat and scratched his head irritably. Mrs. Bunyan saw that she had no hope of getting the judges to summon Bunyan to state his own case, and she burst into tears.

It was not fear or sorrow for herself that brought the tears, but regret for an ugly and cruel world which could not face its own vileness. Thus says that noble woman, the tinker's wife, who showed such dignity and decency in face of Hale's impotent good wishes and Twisden's rancour :

I could not but break forth into tears, not so much because they were so hard-hearted against me and my husband, but to think what a sad account such poor creatures will have to give at the coming of the Lord, when they shall there answer for all things whatsoever they have done in the body, whether it be good or whether it be bad.

TRIAL

Yes, they were poor creatures, all those rich and powerful men of the county, and the two judges, in comparison with the poverty-stricken wife of the tinker.

Notice how frankly and easily she spoke before all the men of her pregnancy and miscarriage. That was the clean, easy manners of a class used to facing the facts of life. Of course she was also speaking in an age still largely free from the pruriency induced by money-fetichism (which, masking all realities of human relationship, inevitably distorts and suppresses sex in every way). Think of, say, a Dickens' heroine in Mrs. Bunyan's predicament. The only woman in a crowd of men—social superiors at that. What horror and fainting-fits the Dickens' heroine would exhibit at the mere thought of talking about pregnancy in such a situation ! This contrast between the clean-minded Mrs. Bunyan and the prurient mid-Victorian girl brings out the vast falsifications of values that had occurred in the intervening two centuries.

15

The Commonwealth

A S we cannot follow out the patterns of thought
and action in Bunyan's work unless we realize
the patterns of history through which he lived, we
must make a brief examination of the Commonwealth. Chiefly we must ask : Why did it fail ?
why was the King restored ? For by answering those
questions we shall discover the basic lines of tension
which finally became intolerable.

But though the Commonwealth broke down, it
had first achieved certain definite results. It had
unshakeably consolidated the bourgeois position.
At the same time, as we have seen, by attacking
the bases of feudalism, it aroused democratic hopes
among the wider masses—hopes which the bourgeois
solution could not satisfy. Cromwell was the leader
of the more active sections of bourgeois and petty-
bourgeois ; he could not, of course, see the struggle
in historical perspective ; but he had a strong sense
of the issues involved. Whenever he came up
against one of the nodal points of class in the clashing
forces of his day, he blazed out into mysticism.
That was the only way he could overcome his sense
of the contradictions involved. Emotionally, there

134

was much of him on the side of the Levellers. But he could not merely say to himself that he rejected the Lilburnean programme as premature ; to overcome the strong attraction he felt for it he had to hide in religious outbursts. The leadership of God that he intuited in those outbursts was the pressure of class-forces demanding so-far-and-no-farther.

His dilemma was roughly this. He saw that if the Lilburnean plan was carried out while England was at such a low state of productivity, with organization so broken and localized, with literacy still confined to so few, the result would be, not to induce progress, but to inhibit it. Half the population, it is estimated, were agricultural labourers ; yeomen made up another sixth. Democracy becomes effective only when the centripedal forces of industrial organization have reached a certain intensity. Before that, the centrifugal tendencies of the petty-bourgeois —the wish to live moated lives of ' self-sufficiency '— impede all developments of technique, all human advance. For the ideal of self-sufficiency is a moral derivative of the small-farm, small-handicraft level of economy. All technical advance involves an increase in socialized methods of production ; it simultaneously draws men closer together and gives them greater power over nature.

Both the Levellers and their opponents knew, and stated, that the achievement of political democracy would mean also an attempt to create economic equality. Such equality, in pre-industrial days, can only mean a sharing-out of the land. That is, a reversion to the ideal of medievalist self-sufficiency.

And that would involve a crash of the political edifice, leading to full-blown feudalism.

In short, Cromwell realized that democracy at this period would mean a setback to economic progress, which would doubly defeat its own end. In the total absence of any scientific method of grasping the problem, he had to fall back on his mystical sense of direction, his intuition of progressive class-pressures. He once asked Ludlow what he wanted. ' That which we fought for ', Ludlow said. ' That the nation might be governed by its consent.' Cromwell answered, ' I am as much for a government by consent as any man, but where shall we find that consent ? '

First, there was the necessary destructive work to be done. To break absolutism and its roots in feudal forms, it was imperative to crush all the monopoly methods which the Crown had been trying to impose on trade and industry. At the same time it was important to carry on effectively the discrediting of gild-corporations. Free-trade was not yet practicable, but the Commonwealth made all the preparations, laid down all the basic lines, from which free-trade could develop. (The term was already quite well known as a slogan.)

The vast sense of freedom that the advent of the Commonwealth brought about appeared in the innumerable schemes of reform. It is no exaggeration to say that almost everything of importance that emerged as a progressive idea during the next two centuries and a half had been anticipated by the theorists of the Commonwealth. The revolutionary ferment made men question all the institutions and ideas they had inertly accepted ; and the result was a marvellously rich stimulus to creative thinking. For when men begin thus to ' question ', they do not abstractly question. They criticize what has so far been done, in the light of the new sense of unity produced by the revolutionary shock. Men of the Commonwealth advocated complete toleration, even for Jews and infidels ; universal suffrage, including suffrage for women ; reform and codification of the laws. They struck out even many of the details of method which later generations would re-discover —penny postage, labour-exchanges, civil marriages, and so on. In ideas on education they were centuries ahead of the generation that followed. Their pro-jected reforms and reconstructions, in short, spanned the whole of the industrial epoch to come, and reached beyond it into the day of socialism.

Yet there was no cohesion. One man, or one section, advocated one idea or set of ideas ; there was no movement which could embrace the whole ferment of thought. For there was no economic basis yet on which to actualize the ideas. The Parliaments of the Commonwealth were singularly futile as far as achievements went ; for the class-forces of the day were in a deadlock. But the political speculation was enormously vital. If one looks at the Barebones Parliament of 1653, made up of ' fanatics ', if one analyses their intentions, their discussions in committee, their conception of what constituted basic issues, one indeed finds them unique in English parliamentary history. They

actually tried to face up to the problem of government in its entirety, and thought nothing of such a
gesture as the offhand abolition of Chancery. They
moved towards the abolition of tithes, civil marriages,
greater efficiency and humaneness all round. And
these were the men elected by the independent
churches. They were incomparably the most progressive parliament, taken in relation to their times,
that England has ever had.

And that was why they failed. That was why
Cromwell failed to set up an enduring Republic.
He and his fellows set up a dictatorship of the
bourgeoisie. So have Hitler and Mussolini. The
contrast between these two dictatorships shows us
how dangerous it is to use terms abstractly ; and
we use them abstractly the moment we fail to fill
them up with their historical content. The bourgeoisie that Cromwell led were moving into toleration
and free-trade ; and in this first impact of their
success it was the generous and constructive side
that came uppermost.

Cromwell had crushed Lilburne because his intuition of history, of God, made him realize that
Lilburne's project, however worthy, could only
have the effect of doing the exact opposite of what
Lilburne wanted. But having defeated Lilburne,
he in turn wanted to build as stably as he could
on the historical class-forces that he had intuitively
accepted as blessed. He now wanted justice within
those limits. He spoke as strongly about the
oppressions of the law as did Lilburne himself. He saw that unless some stand was made

against the enclosings it was a mockery to talk of justice.

He thus found himself in a position with certain similarities to that of Charles I. As Laud had attacked enclosure because he wanted *all* classes kept in their place, so Cromwell (during the brief period when England was under his Major-Generals) in 1655–6 tried to hold the enclosures up.[1] But whereas Laud had been facing towards the medieval age, Cromwell was facing towards the modern democratic.

The difficulty that faced him was to find a way of establishing a collaboration between big and petty bourgeois, as he had established it during the Civil War. That way was not evident : it was non-existent. What beat him was the deepening conflict between the small and the big landowners, the journeymen and their trade-masters, the small traders and the big companies. Everywhere the same division was showing up. The journeymen were making the last fight to control the masters within the gild-organization ; they were crushed. A more determined fight in the Common Council of London won a temporary democratic victory. But there was no means of welding all these forces in a ' national unity '

So, baffled at home, Cromwell turned outwards his sense of unity. He dreamed of a great Protestant Union of Europe. This dream was partly born of a

---

[1] Sir Ralph Verney writes at this time, ' I confess I love old England very well, but as things are carried here the gentry cannot joy much to be in it '.

failure to realize that the early days of Protestantism were past. In those days, when the reactionary triumph of the Papacy was always possible, all Protestant groups felt a certain solidarity of interests. Once the Papacy was decisively beaten, then the Protestant groups found how strong were their own rivalries. The astonished faces of the Dutch representatives, to whom Cromwell broached his scheme, expressed their recognition of this simple fact. But Cromwell, to escape the insuperable difficulties of his internal policy, was forced to cling to his dream. He fought his Spanish wars because of it, and almost ruined English trade. Not that there were only destructive results ; he had set England up as a power to be respected—'He made us Freemen of the Continent', wrote Dryden—and he had given a powerful impetus to imperialist ambitions. But for the moment he miscalculated. The City of London had opposed the break with Spain, for trade reasons ; and the City had the last word. In 1658–9 the contradictions of his policy resulted in an economic crisis. The Restoration of the Stuarts was assured.

The bourgeois wanted the King because they saw that only the rule of kingship could provide them with the screen most satisfactory at that stage. The Dutch had a Republic, and had long been the leading commercial nation ; but the inner weakness of their federated forms (inevitable where so many 'interests' had equal power) was now showing itself. The English bourgeoisie followed a sound intuition when they plumped for the Restoration.

THE COMMONWEALTH

They must have known that the struggle with absolutism would begin afresh ; but they felt that this time they would be fighting on ground enormously more to their advantage than in 1642. They were right ; for when the clash did come again in twenty-eight years time, they were able to chase the King out like any ordinary defaulter. Thenceforward the Crown remained essentially their pawn—George III's movement towards absolutism being sufficiently crippled by the American Revolution.

But meanwhile, in 1660, what the bourgeoisie wanted above all things was to have a sympathetically-oppressive state which would allow them to make the fullest business use of the civil-war gains and to crush the democratic manifestations which Cromwell tolerated and in so many ways encouraged. Therefore they wanted the King back. In the last resort Cromwell's humanism had been impeding the productive advance, though the Commonwealth was of inestimable value as a period of anti-feudalist consolidation.

Among the many reasons, the bourgeois wanted the King back so that they might put such men as John Bunyan in prison.

16

In Prison

OF the County Jail in which Bunyan was imprisoned only a massive door of three layers
of oak, fastened through with iron bolts, and barred
across an open centre, now remains. We know,
however, that there were two floors, a small court-
yard, and iron-grated windows looking out on the
Jail Lane, or Silver Street side, from which prisoners
used to hang out bags or purses for alms. There
were also dungeons underground. In the eighteenth
century we hear that the ground floor, with two day
rooms and some sleeping-rooms, was kept for felons ;
the upper floor, with four bedrooms and one com-
mon-room (also used as chapel), was kept for
debtors. Clearly, as there were sometimes as many
as sixty dissenters imprisoned, besides debtors and
felons, the place must have been very cramped and
miserable, even if not so foul and heart-rending as
many of the prisons of the day.

We find a prisoner from this jail petitioning in
1666 (when Bunyan was still there) that ' he hath
suffered as much misery as so dismal a place could
be capable to inflict, and so is likely to perish without His Majesty's further compassion and mercy
towards him '. In another plea he speaks of ' a

calamitous condition '. We may take it that there were beds of straw, no fireplaces, and a general insanitary state of dirt, with continual cases of jail-fever. We may take it also that all the prisoners would have been lousy.

Bunyan never had any complaint about his physical sufferings. Like a brave man, he admits to fear. He thought he would be hanged, and he feared that he would make a ' scrabbling shift ' when he had to climb the ladder, and would thus shame his cause with a pale face and tottering knees. He suffered from being cut off from the work which he had felt a worthy service of humanity. He suffered from being torn away from family and children. It was ' as the pulling of the flesh from my bones ' when he was parted from them. And the thought of the privations and sorrows he must cause them by his struggle struck a deep wound. Especially he suffered at the thought of his blind girl's misery. For she ' lay nearer my heart than all I had besides ; O the thoughts of the hardship I thought my Blind one might go under, would break my heart to pieces '. But he could not leave the cause. ' Recalling myself, thought I, I must venture you all with God, though it goeth to the quick to leave you. O, I saw in this condition I was a man who was pulling down his house upon the head of his wife and children. Yet, thought I, I must do it, I must do it.'

And that settled it. Having made his decision, he was not one to whine about it. He went into the dirty jail, and for twelve years was an imprisoned man.

At first, during the Autumn and Spring Assizes, when he was trying to get his name inserted in the calendar of prisoners for trial, he had a certain amount of liberty allowed him ; but his enemies soon learned of this, threatened to indict the jailer and tried to have him dismissed, and Bunyan was straitly held.

He was a poor man, with no reserve of resources ; the congregation to which he belonged was poor ; he could expect little help. He earned a certain amount of money by making grosses of tagged laces in the jail ; but this method of employment could not have kept him and his family. Doubtless his wife found some kind of work for herself and the children. When he did get out of jail he found ' his temporal affairs were gone to wreck ', and he had to begin them again as if he had newly come into the world. One takes this to mean that whatever small property he had accumulated out of his earnings had been sold, and that he had lost whatever regular custom he had as a brazier.

But, though the lack of liberty must have been a sore weight for a man so energetically minded and bodied, so used to the wandering life of a tinker, there was not a complete cessation of contact with the activities that meant so much to him. Other dissenters came and went as fellow-prisoners ; sometimes there was a big catch and he had plenty of godly companionship ; once at least he had two ejected rectors with him. He had his two books, the Bible and Foxe's *Martyrs*. And doubtless he was allowed a fair number of visitors. We hear of a woman from a neighbouring town who came to put before him her case of conscience ; and when there were fellow-dissenters in jail, they could hold services. He tells us of one such occasion. It was usual for each man to speak something for the 'edification' of the group ; but Bunyan, when his turn came, felt 'empty, spiritless and barren'. Then, at last, he saw in the chapter of the Bible before him 'something of that jasper in whose light you there find this holy city is said to come or descend'. And he burst out into eloquence, which he later transcribed as a book, *The Holy City*. It was natural that the city of incorruptible stones should beam with glory for him in his prison of grimy and insanitary gloom.

In 1664 the persecution of dissenters became acute. It is of interest to note how the bourgeoisie were now as virulent against dissent as ever the feudalist Laud had been. Now it was the King, with his tendency towards absolutism and the wish to aid the Catholics, who was trying to introduce toleration. Here we see the same dilemma as we saw when Laud was more sincere and keen in stopping enclosures than were the bourgeois upholders of 'liberty'. Charles II or Laud was not actuated by anything progressive. Each wished to preserve a 'balance', so that all classes might be kept subservient. It was the enclosing and intolerant bourgeois who were driving ahead.

The bourgeois intolerance of dissent expressed the split that had come ever since Lilburne raised the banner of the Levellers. If the bourgeois were doing the work of history by lifting the standard of productivity, so were the dissenters doing that work by opposing the bourgeois block. The dissenting protest shows the gathering of the working-class forces that were ultimately to unite under the banner of trade-unions and socialism. *Then* the division which had so tormented Bunyan was healed. The abstraction of the Birthright returned to the revolutionary fact which Birthright had been in the idiom of Lilburne.

The abstraction of the Birthright, the religious formulation in which Bunyan stands supreme, was, then, we see, the necessary expression for the period when out of vast confused suffering and uprooting the industrial proletariat was being created.

It was the only form in which the sense of unity could be compacted and carried on through a period of transition, when organization for the workers was impossible.

But in his prison Bunyan had a consolation. The decision that he had taken, to suffer all things without complaint for the unity that he felt in him, intensified his mental power. The privations, sexual and otherwise, became the test of his physical discipline. He had been a notable preacher in an age when there were many notable preachers. Now his full powers flashed forth ; and he wrote his autobiography, *Grace Abounding*. I have sought to show how profoundly this book mirrors the crisis of its day. But there can be no question as to the skill and insight with which Bunyan reconstructs the history of his conversion. Nothing is more difficult than to recall the stages of such a process ; for the blinding light of revelation with which it ends is also a total revaluation of life. Consequently one can only after many arduous efforts of memory get back to the earlier modes and values of one's thought. The new light is so intense that one's past struggles lose their reality ; one cannot understand what it was that kept holding one back from the realization that now seems so obvious, so overpowering.

Bunyan's triumph of discipline lies in the power he shows to objectify his past struggle, to build it up stage by stage exactly as it occurred. Of course he can make this reconstruction only from within the ideology of the struggle. It is not to be expected that (supposing my analysis of the social reality behind his conflict to be correct) he could see what were the objective historical factors from which his personal conflict derived ; but he has an astonishing capacity to revive the memories of each stage of his conflict and to give a connected series, a dramatically just definition, of the states of being through which he passed.

Yes, he felt that he had his reward for constancy. ' I never had in all life so great an inlet into the Word of God as now.' Everything shone with a new clarity, a new depth of meaning. The preface of *Grace Abounding* is a trumpet-call of strength and confidence.

I now once again, as before, from the top of Shenir and Hermon, so now from the lions' dens, from the mountains of the leopards, do look yet after you all, greatly longing to see your safe arrival into the desired haven. I thank God upon every remembrance of you ; and rejoice, even while I stick between the teeth of the lions in the wilderness.

Here we have the authentic class-voice of the dispossessed, who abide their time, who are ready to take suffering and contempt and outrage, knowing that out of this resolute acceptance there will be bred the powers of active resistance when the time arrives. *Hold fast till I come.* Those are the last words of *The Holy War.* The Redeemer speaks them. As long as this stout-hearted trust and defiance remain, the hope of the future remains. It is revolutionary energy driven inward. And so we see that Bunyan's long and agonized abstraction and inversion of the revolutionary ideas of his age was not a fruitless thing : it was part of the process whereby the emotional core of those ideas might be preserved through the dark days of unavoidable oppression.

Remember also your tears and prayers to God ; yea, how you sighed under every hedge for mercy. Have you never a hill Mizar to remember ? Have you forgot the close, the milk house, the stable, the barn, and the like, where God did visit your soul ? Remember also the Word— the Word, I say, upon which the Lord hath caused you to hope. If you have sinned against light ; if you are tempted to blaspheme ; if you are down in despair ; if you think God fights against you ; or if heaven is hid from your eyes, remember it was thus with your father, but out of them all the Lord delivered me.

The book appeared in 1666, published by George Larkin of London, a bookseller who suffered much in the cause of free expression, being once jailed for ' having a hand in printing and compiling dangerous books '. He was often raided, and we hear of a raid in 1666 when, among other books, those of Bunyan were seized.

IN PRISON

About the time when *Grace Abounding* appeared,
Bunyan was let out of prison. A later writer said that
' some in trust and power ' pitied and interceded for
him ; more likely the Plague had demoralized the
prison arrangements. For the Plague had spread
into the countryside from London, and we hear of
forty deaths from it at Bedford. Then came the
further demoralization following the Fire of London.
And Clarendon, the arch-reactionary, was losing his
grip.

But whatever its causes, the release was of little use
to Bunyan. He at once began preaching again ; and
before six weeks were out he was arrested at a meeting
and put back into the jail.

For six more years he remained in that miserable
confinement, uncomplaining. But he seems to have
lost something of his resilience. He had written
nine books during the first six years ; he wrote only
two during the next six. And the second of those
two was written in a short period immediately before
his release in 1672.

He had made a great effort to use the new insight
generated by his conviction of suffering for the cause,
and he had put himself with a masterly fullness into
Grace Abounding. But after that he felt himself
temporarily exhausted. The effort to fight the depression of endless captivity took up all his time ;
but he was also storing within himself the energy for
a new outburst.

During 1668 there was a slackening in persecution,
owing to seventeen months' adjournment of Parliament. At once there was an awakening in dissenting

149

activity. 'The separatists increase daily', wrote a
Bedford vicar in a letter. 'God amend all things in
the nation.' The Free Church sprang back into life,
though some of its members had fallen away and con-
formed to the national Church. (We may note how
in this question of fighting the 'national Church' is
expressed the subtle relation between the Law from
which Grace redeemed, and the actual repressive laws
of class-society.) Bunyan was able to partake once
more of church activities, probably with the con-
nivance of the jailers. We find an under-jailer presented for refusing to pay the church-rate. If he was
one of Bunyan's converts he was not made of his
master's stern stuff, for he caved in and paid after all.
But in April 1670 Parliament re-enacted the Conventicle Act, and there was another outburst of violent
repression.

An examination of the accused shows the class-
basis of dissent. A sprinkling of esquires, gentlemen,
yeomen, and farmers were caught by the sense of a
fuller life in the dissenters' idiom ; but the mass of
the sufferers were artisans and workers—cordwainers,
fellmen, weavers, warreners, gardeners, fullers, dressers
of hemp, farm-labourers, ploughwrights, cobblers,
maltsters, and their like.

A pamphlet gives us a detailed picture of a raid on
the Bedford Nonconformists ; and the story is worth
re-telling. These men were fighting for a narrow
creed. But that narrow creed was an explosive blast-
ing the way into the future. Historically, it was a
fight for freedom ; and these humble men and women
of Bedford were making possible our own fight.

17

Repression

ON 11 April the New Conventicles Act was passed.
Sunday 15 May the Bedford authorities struck.
The dissenters were meeting at the house of John
Fenn, haberdasher. Two apparitors, with a warrant
from Mr. Foster, J.P., entered the house and forced
the meeters along to Foster's house in Well Street
Ward. Foster (the lawyer who came in with the
candle at Harlington House) fined them one and all
according to what he considered their property-
status, and committed to prison the man who had
been preaching.

Next Friday, one Battison, a churchwarden, went
round to levy the fines. He started at John Bardolf's
malthouse. Bardolf had expected him and had
purposely sold all his malt. The legal point arose
whether the officers had the right to break open the
malthouse door when the malt was no longer Bardolf's.
An indignant crowd had gathered ; and while the
officers were talking, somebody fixed a calf's tail to
Battison's back. The crowd mocked Battison and
howled him off the premises.

The officers then went to Edward Covington, a
grocer. His wife had been fined five shillings.
Covington refused to pay. Battison saw a brass

kettle, and seized it for the fine. When he appeared with it at the front door, the crowd jeered, and the other officers refused to take it. At last Battison found a boy who agreed to carry the kettle to an inn-yard for sixpence. The crowd followed, hooting ; and the innkeeper refused to allow the boy to take the kettle into the yard. As the boy dropped the kettle, the innkeeper made his man take it out into the middle of the street.

The first day's distraints were thus rather un-successful.

Next day, which was market day, the Justices took steps to see that things were done with the violence necessary to overawe the populace. They com-manded the officers to smash down doors and levy the distresses. While the market was in full swing, Battison, with a file of soldiers and the constables, marched off to Bardolf's malthouse, which stood in an inn yard in the middle of the market-place. They broke down the doors and distrained fourteen quarters of malt.

Undeterred, the dissenters met next day, Sunday, as if nothing had happened. Battison, with the appari-tors and another warrant from Foster, pushed his way into the meeting about nine o'clock in the morning. The meeters refused to budge till their exercise was ended, unless he carried them all off by force. Battison sent word to Foster. Foster replied with orders to arrest the whole gathering and gave a list of gentlemen of the town who would render assistance. Battison went off to collect these gentlemen, with a crowd of about a hundred watching him.

REPRESSION

By ten o'clock Battison had his force assembled. He rounded up the meeters and drove them to the Swan Inn. There they were kept till four in the afternoon. The justices took their names and then they were let go.

Next day Foster himself took charge of the distraining. With old Battison, two apparitors, the constables, and a file of soldiers, he started on the rounds. He tried to add to his force by charging to his assistance various men he met. Others he sent for. But very few obeyed his call. Most of the tradesmen, journeymen, labourers, and servants had gone out of the town or hid themselves ; there was scarcely anyone in the town. Bedford looked like a deserted village. The shops were all shut down, as if a plague-warning had been issued.

First Foster came to the house of Nicholas Hawkins, cutler. The children there were sick of the smallpox. Likewise at the house of Thomas Honeylove, shoemaker. Afraid of smallpox, Foster did not linger at these houses. But at Michael Shepherd's he got five shillings. Then he came to the house of Thomas Cooper, heelmaker, whose fine was forty shillings. He distrained three cartloads of wood which had been specially cut for Cooper's heel-making work and was worth more than all his household goods put together. As Cooper was a very poor man, living only upon making heels and lasts, we may presume that he was now ruined.

Daniel Rich, tanner, had his best coat taken away, against a fine of five shillings imposed on his wife. John Spencer, grocer, lost shop-goods against a forty-shilling fine. Jay the baker was then plundered. Then the blacksmith Isaac was deprived of his locks, shovels, and the very anvil on which he was working.

Next Foster went to Thomas Arthur, pipe-maker. The door was locked, but Arthur opened as soon as the officers knocked. Foster demanded £11. Arthur asked to see the warrant. It was for £6. Foster answered that a further £5 was charged on account of the locked door. Arthur, seeing that all his goods would be distrained, cried, ' Sir, what shall my children do? shall they starve? '

Foster replied that while he was a rebel his children should starve. And next Wednesday Battison with apparitors, musketeers, and a cart, carried away all the household goods they thought fit to take, and all the wood that Arthur had collected for his work—three cart-loads—not even leaving enough for a kiln of pipes that he had ready set. Arthur pleaded for mercy, and some of the men accompanying Battison took his part ; but Battison had his orders and knew Mr. Foster, J.P.

Meanwhile the Monday's distraints went on. Robert Brown, gardener, was mulcted of £3. Mrs. Mary Tilney, widow, had to pay £20 ; and Foster informed her that he would make an example of her and attend personally with his Public Notary to see her goods carried off. Which he later did. They took her tables, cupboards, chairs, irons, feather-beds, blankets, the room-hangings, the sheets off her bed. The value of the goods was between £40 and £50. Mrs. Tilney comforted her poor neighbours who kept weeping and wailing. She herself maintained her cheerfulness. Mr. Foster, J.P., satisfied with the day's work, now went home to dine.

Next day, Tuesday, more fines were levied. Battison, with constables and soldiers, marched up High Street. John Fenn, haberdasher, a good friend of Bunyan, was to pay £5. So all the stock of hats and hat-bands was taken away out of his shop ; and next day his household goods were taken. After John Fenn, his brother Samuel, also a hatter, was dealt with.

So it went on, day after day. From one parish to the next. From Bedford to Cotten End. At Cotten End Sir George Blundell joined Foster in the work of repression. Thorogood the weaver, at whose house meetings were held, had all the implements of his trade taken away, against a £19 fine. Impoverished, he and his wife left the house. Weaver lost his loom, and farmer lost his cows ; and the people cheerfully went on with their belief that life under the Law was evil and only life under grace could redeem. We do not wonder when we find that Bunyan can say no worse of anyone than that he has a ' legal mind '.

18

Pastor of the Flock

THE spy-system was excellent. For instance, the Government had a book dealing with the district between Bedford and Cambridge, in which all suspects were alphabetically listed, places of meeting and lurking-holes were detailed, and the routes of the illegal preachers were given. There had been spies at work ever since the Law of Uniformity ; but in 1670–71 there was a boom in the trade.

Bunyan tells us of one W. S., who was William Swinton, sexton of a Bedford church. An earnest spy, Swinton used to sneak about in the dark, climb trees, and crawl through the woods in the daytime to catch any dissenter-gathering in the open fields. The tale went that Swinton fell from the bell in the steeple-house and was picked up all bloody, dying. Another informer, says Bunyan, at St. Neot's was bitten by a dog and died of gangrene, rotting away. And another, Fecknam, Swinton's pal, a spendthrift, died raving a month after harrying the meeters in John Fenn's house.

Signs perhaps that the Almighty—the irresistible force of human history—was quietly getting ready the vengeances that would some day sweep the Swintons and the Fosters off the earth. The day of judgment.

Near the end of 1673 the question of electing Bunyan to the position of pastor came to the fore ; and on 21 January 1672 he was elected ' by the solemn lifting up of their hands '. The lack of a pastor had weakened the efficiency of the church ; and we may be sure that it was only the enforced absence of Bunyan in prison which had delayed his election till this late date. John Fenn was elected deacon at the same time.

Seven weeks later came the Declaration of Indulgence—an act of the royal prerogative overriding law—and Bunyan was enabled shortly afterwards to take up his pastorate. He received in May a licence to preach, and for £50 the congregation purchased a barn off Mill Lane, which was turned into a church.

Bunyan signalized his release by a very energetic campaign of preaching, not only in Bedford and in the countryside round about, but also in places such as Gamlingay and Ashwell in the neighbouring counties. We even hear of him at Leicester. There are many traditions of his preaching-places in Bedfordshire, cottage or farmhouse, or a green dell in a thick wood near Preston Castle—a fine spot for Nonconformist gatherings, since it was capable of holding several hundred people sheltered, while scouts guarded the approaches.

We may note in passing that Bunyan, strict though he was on the question of grace, was by no means a dogmatic Baptist. In his writings he deprecates the making of baptism a controversial question ; and he had his son Joseph, born in 1672,[1] baptised in a Bedford parish church. (Perhaps, however, he did this merely as an act of civic conformity, a matter of registration, not considering that it involved his principles.) He was in his tenets an Independent with a Calvinist attitude. The services in the converted barn must have been very simple in form ; there was no singing and no pronouncing of a blessing by the minister at the end.

From the church records we learn the kind of things that took up the attention of the pastor and the other church leaders. A man who got so drunk that he was carried home senseless was cast out of the congregation. A sister was admonished for neglecting communion and countenancing cardplay, even teaching her children the games. A girl was rebuked for calling her father a liar and for ' wicked carriages to her mother '. Another girl kept immodest company ' with carnal and light young fellows at Elstow '. And another girl slept several nights in the same room as a young man, when there was no one else in the house. And of course there were backsliders and makers of division.

A small kingdom, but sufficient to give the sense of having a concrete area in which to exercise judgement, election, power, apart from the class-state.

In February 1674 occurred an episode which,

[1] This boy was baptized on 16 November. Bunyan was not formally released till September, but was certainly out of jail by May. On 27 March he was still in prison, for he dated a book on that day ' From Prison '. But he must have already had some means of having intercourse with his wife.

thought slight in itself, might have had serious consequences.

At Edworth, near the Hertfordshire border, lived a farmer, John Beaumont. He was a widower, and his daughter Agnes, aged twenty-three, kept house for him. There was a son and another daughter, but they were married and lived in other farms near by. The son John was a dissenter who had incurred a fine in 1669 ; and the father had himself been under the spell of Bunyan's preaching. ' And afterwards ', says Agnes, ' would cry to the Lord in secret as well as I '. But some neighbours, whose opinion carried weight with him, managed to prejudice his mind against Bunyan.

Agnes had joined the Bedford Church at Gamlingay ; and in February 1674 she wanted very much to attend a service there. Reluctantly her father agreed. In the morning she went over to call on her brother and made arrangements to meet him and some others. She was to ride pillion behind one John Wilson. Wilson for some reason failed to arrive ; and the brother was taking his wife on his own horse. He couldn't spare another horse from farm-work, the February roads were too slushy for walking, and so Agnes was stranded.

' Oh ', said Agnes to herself, ' that God would please put it in the heart of somebody to come this way and carry me, and make some way or other for my going '. She waited, full of trepidation. Then who should appear but Bunyan himself. He was on his way to the meeting and called in at the brother's house. Agnes was overjoyed, but doubtful if she could win the enormous favour of actually riding behind the master. She whispered to her brother, and he said to Bunyan, ' I desire you to carry my sister behind you '.

Bunyan answered very roughly, ' No, not I. I will not carry her '. He knew of her father's prejudice, and in any event it was not seemly for a pastor to ride about with young girls clinging to him.

These were cutting words of his, thought Agnes, and she wept bitterly. Her brother pleaded for her : ' If you do not carry her, you will break her heart '.

Bunyan answered as before. He would not take her. Turning to Agnes, he added, ' If I should carry you, your father would be grievous angry with me '.

Agnes replied, ' If you please to carry me, I will venture that '.

Her brother upheld her, and after many entreaties Bunyan agreed. Agnes climbed up behind him. ' Oh, how glad I was that I was going ! ' But she had scarcely started off, when her father came hurrying over to his son's farm. He saw the party as it disappeared, and asked some of the farm-labourers who was the horseman carrying his daughter. They told him it was Bunyan. He fell into a passion and ran down to the close end, hoping to intercept the riders. In his rage he meant to pull Agnes off the horse. But the riders had already passed. Agnes was unaware of her father's pursuit, taken up with her pride at being mounted with the master.

' To speak the truth ', says Agnes, ' I had not gone far, behind him, but my heart was puffed up with pride, and I began to have high thoughts of myself and proud to think I should ride behind such a man as he was ; and I was pleased that anybody did look after me as I rode along. And sometimes he would be speaking to me about the things of God, as we went along. And indeed I thought myself a happy body that day ; first that it did so please God to make way for my going to the meeting, and then that I should have the honour to ride behind him. But, as you will understand, my pride had a fall.'

The meeting was duly held ; but at the end of it Bunyan could not give her a ride home. When at last she did get back that night, her father had locked the door and gone to bed. Agnes had to spend the night, a chilly February night, in the barn in her riding-clothes. Next morning her father remained obdurate and refused to have anything to do with her. He even threatened to cut her out of his will unless she promised not to go again to one of Bunyan's meetings without permission. There was a worried week, which Agnes spent in her brother's house. Next Sunday she decided to submit to her father, and returned home.

Two days later, on Tuesday, when she and her father were alone in the house, he had a seizure of some kind and died. The same day a clergyman named Lane was spreading scandal about her at Baldock Fair. Lane, though preaching at Edworth, lived at Bedford. He had recognized Bunyan and his pillion-girl, and told how he had seen them riding together. His suggestion that Agnes was Bunyan's mistress mixed with the news of the quarrel between

Agnes and her father, and her father's sudden death, to produce a tale in which Agnes had poisoned her father to get revenge and to hide her unchastity. A lawyer named Farrow, who had vainly wooed Agnes, was the chief venter of this tale. He added that Bunyan had provided the poison.

It was a frightening moment; for accusations of poison were difficult to disprove in days of immature medical science. However, an investigation was made, which was considered to prove that John Beaumont had died a natural death; and so the matter ended. Agnes lived till 1720. She penned an account of this episode with Bunyan, which explains why he added in a new edition of *Grace Abounding* a passionate rejection of the charge of sexual immorality. People were saying, he says, that he had his misses, his whores, his bastards—yea, two wives at once, and the like. He swears that he knows no woman breathing except his wife, 'but by their apparel, their children, or by common fame'. He shrinks even from the usual greeting kiss. He seldom allows himself to touch even a woman's hand.

Two sentences of this outburst are of interest:

When they have used to the utmost of their endeavours, and made the fullest inquiry that they can, to prove against me truly, that there is any woman in heaven, or earth, or hell, that can say I have at any time, in any place, by day or night, so much as attempted to be naught with them; and speak I thus, to beg mine enemies into a good esteem of me? no, not I: I will in this beg relief of no man; believe or disbelieve me in this, all is a case to me.

This sentence is very confusedly put, and shows a

strong perturbation. I do not mean to suggest that Bunyan is lying ; I am sure he was incapable of a lie. But one feels a physical agitation of some kind in it, which is perhaps illuminated by a later remark, ' I admire the wisdom of God, that he made me shy of women from my first conversion until now '. This definitely suggests that he had not been shy before his conversion.

In February 1675 preachers' warrants were revoked by royal proclamation. Bunyan's enemies at once seized the chance. On 4 March a warrant was issued for his arrest. Foster, the familiar persecutor, was active in this. He was an ecclesiastical lawyer, a diocesan chancellor and a commissary. Bunyan was arrested and placed, not in the county jail, but in the town jail on the seven-spanned Bedford Bridge. On each side of the central arch was a tower-gateway, that to the north having the jail, that to the south the magazine and county storehouse. An upper chamber on the east side of the north tower was used for the jail ; beneath it was a stair of stone leading down to an island-strip green with shrubs.

It was in this cramped space, above the sound of running water, that Bunyan got the idea for *The Pilgrim's Progress* ; and before he was released after six months' imprisonment he had written at least a large portion of the allegory. The two external impacts that contributed to this resurrection of literary creativeness in Bunyan were, firstly, the fresh shock of being imprisoned once more after the few years of enhanced activity ; and secondly, the fact that old Thomas Bunyan, John's father, died in the same month as the revoking of licences occurred. The death of a father is an event that affects anyone strongly ; for in class-society the discords which we have analysed make the father the image of all authority, so that his death forces the son sharply up against all the discords, social and personal, which strive to rend the individual's sense of worth and responsibility. And we have seen what a dark sense of blood-guilt Bunyan had had to fight. Certainly he had fought out that fight and resolved it on a higher level at his conversion ; but enough of the old fear must have remained to make his father's death a shock. Thomas left a will in which he gave each of his four children, one of whom was John, a shilling ; the rest of his belongings he left to his wife Anne. He had, then, been on friendly terms with his son, the successful and persecuted preacher ; but the tensions which we have analysed as existing in earlier years would have been revived by the event of his death.

19

'The Pilgrim's Progress'

BUNYAN had probably read a fair number of books in a scattered way. For instance, in the treatise written just before *The Pilgrim's Progress* we can detect that he has been reading some of the Books of Characters, such as Earle's. The use of dialogue in one of the books that he mentions as brought by his first wife had also probably affected him. But it is pointless work to search through the various books of devotions or emblems that he might have read, to find the ' sources ' of his allegory. The idea of the Christian life as a pilgrimage would have reached him through various channels ; and the trick of personifying sins and virtues and states of mind was common to the whole period. Its roots in popular literature went back to the old interludes ; we see it, mixed up with the notion that variations of character represented quantitative variations of certain fixed humours, in the comedies of Ben Jonson ; we see it again in the Puritan assumption of names that were felt to express the (actual or desired) virtues of the possessor. But though there were no literary ' sources ' for Bunyan's book, it sprang from a deeply-based tradition. It links up with medieval allegory through the unbroken tradition of the popular pulpit. Here, from the breasts of a living popular tradition of style and thought, Bunyan drew the milk of his inspiration. The simple directness of the medieval pulpit-style, its way of figuring intellectual and moral ideas in concretely personalized form, its use of homely metaphor and illustration—these elements had continued through the centuries, outside the modes of the written book. The popular pulpit in Bunyan's day still maintained this tradition. The popular sermon was based in medieval tradition, unlike the sermons of the learned divines that found their way into print.

The whole schemata of Bunyan's allegories can be traced back to medieval pulpit allegory. The most remarkable anticipation of his Pilgrim allegory is to be found in a vernacular treatise on the *Way to Paradise* written about the end of the fourteenth century or early fifteenth. Here we have the Pilgrim with ' a great sack on his shoulders ' ; and his efforts to keep to the strait path and to avoid the Slough are described in terms often almost identical with Bunyan's. Yet there is no doubt that Bunyan had no direct contact with this or any other medieval homilectic allegory. What the medieval parallels interestingly show is that the stream of imagery had flowed undisturbed down to Bunyan's day in the popular pulpit. We know of one puritan preacher, Thomas Adams, who in 1612 was preaching at Willington, only half-an-hour's walk from Elstow, and whose sermons were in the true medieval vein.

The idea that Bunyan was to develop in *The Holy War* was again an idea extremely common in medieval homilectic : that of the soul as a castle suffering incessant besieges and attacks. ' Man's soul ', says a fifteenth-century English preacher, is ' a city defended and besieged '. Bunyan in his two allegories is thus merely taking up commonplaces of medieval thought and re-clothing them in terms of his own experience.[1]

But it is this re-clothing that is the important matter. The medieval soul is merely besieged endlessly in terms of the incessant feudal warfare of the day. Bunyan's Mansoul is a reflection of society in the throes of manifest transition. His Pilgrim is no longer a soul abstracted amid eternal vicissitudes seeking an eternal home, an escape from pointlessly repeated cruelties and oppressions. He is the petty-bourgeois dissenter with a job to do. Bunyan's contribution to the popular images and themes that he accepts from the tradition is to be found in the historically-realistic precision, the concrete adaptation to a new feeling of social process. And it is that new direction and concretion which is the significant part. Yet we must note that the great power of his work, the tremendous capacity it had to affect his generation and the following generations of dissenters, lay in the fact that it concentrated the ideas and images of a whole vast body of popular literature—the body which had for centuries alone been close to the living needs of men and women, close to the mass-needs.

[1] The idea of the dream-vision is directly in line with the great medieval allegories such as *Piers Plowman*, *Pearl*, *Roman de la Rose*. Bunyan could not have known this. His use of the Dream is merely another instance of the way he unconsciously resumes the whole medieval apparatus of allegory.

Bunyan thus takes up the medieval basis and transforms it to the requirements of the new epoch. The most original work of literature is that which most deeply and widely resumes, in terms of a new social sense, the themes and imageries that have developed out of mass-needs. Bunyan is thus essentially original. His book-sources are slight ; his sources in popular culture are enormous. It was this balance of extreme individual originality and profound mass-content that moved the detractors of his day to insist that he must have plagiarized. He was so original that they felt sure he must have copied.

In all that we say, then, of Bunyan's creative originality, his definition of his own age in his work, we must remember that there underlies his originality the resumption of a great mass-culture developed through the pulpit of many centuries.

The ' Christian Life ' is the theme. Which in fact means the life of John Bunyan, tinker, who soldiered through the Civil War, represented in terms of Christian imagery. Whereas in *Grace Abounding* he had sought to recall and re-state the various pressures and patterns of thought and feeling through which he had passed on his way to conversion, now he sought to use the religious imagery as a means of getting at the inner meaning of his struggle, its dramatic immediacy.

Before we deal at length with his achievement, we will take a brief synopsis of the allegory as a sketch-map for our inquiry.

Christian, faced with world-end terror, sets out for his salvation, abandoning his wife and children, at the advice of Evangelist. Neighbour Pliable goes with him. They meet the Slough of Despond, and Pliable turns back. Mr. Worldly Wisdom tries to divert the Pilgrim, who is later put right by Evangelist. The Pilgrim reaches the wicket-gate, where Good Will awaits him. Directed, he finds the house of Interpreter. Thence he comes to the foot of the Cross, where his burden drops off.

He passes Simple, Sloth, and Presumption ; meets Formalist and Hypocrite ; and climbs Hill Difficulty, where he loses his roll in an arbour. He passes lions, comes to the Palace Beautiful. There he is welcomed by Discretion ; entertained by Prudence, Piety, and Charity ; lodged in the room of Peace ; and armoured. So he goes down into the Valley of Humiliation, where he fights and defeats the fiend Apollyon.

Then he passes through the Valley of the Shadow of Death. He gains Faithful as his companion ; passes the caverns of the giants Pope and Pagan ; meets Talkative, and then Evangelist once more. He and Faithful come to Vanity Fair. Faithful is arrested, tried, and slain. The Pilgrim gets away ; gains Hopeful as his companion ; meets By-ends ; passes Demas and his silver mine, and Lot's transformed wife ; goes along a pleasant river ; enters Doubting Castle of Giant Despair. Released by the key of promise, he escapes, and comes to the Delectable Mountains and their kindly Shepherds, who show him a hell-mouth of deceit, of which to beware. He meets Ignorance ; tells the story of Little Faith, who was waylaid near by ; meets Flatterer with his net and

Atheist with his laugh ; passes over the Enchanted Ground and reaches the Country of Beulah. The Celestial City is now near. But the River has yet to be crossed. The Pilgrims, Christian and Hopeful, cross successfully; but Ignorance is thrust down a hole into hell at the last moment.

Such is the story, dryly and briefly told. There are several aspects of it that we must treat. First we will notice how closely this apparently generalized narrative is bound up with Bunyan's direct place-memories. It is worth considering the points of reference, for they reveal how intimately Bunyan read himself into the allegory. It is this intimacy which gives the book its creative force.

Beyond doubt Bunyan had a deep feeling for Nature. Even in *Grace Abounding*, where the inner conflict so obsesses him, we are again and again made to feel how his mental struggle is entangled with the scenes among which he lives. Therefore, when he turns to a dramatization of his struggle, he inevitably places it among the lanes and hills where he fought out the strife of ideas. The Pilgrim fighting across the fabulous landscape of salvation is very clearly the tinker with wildly-stirred brain trudging the Bedfordshire roads—with his tinker's wallet on his back, as Christian had his Burden.

The Slough of Despond, for instance, lies north of Dunstable on the Hockley Road, where a steep slope leads down to a quaggy vale. Though the road was much travelled, it was allowed to remain in a very boggy state. Celia Fiennes, in her diary, 1695, remarks, ' Seven miles over a sad road, called Hockley

in the Hole, as full of deep sloughs as in the winter
it must be impassable '. The River Ouse began here,
all the surface-water draining down from the sides of
the downs. Bunyan allegorizes this fact as the descent
of the scum and filth attending sin.

The House of the Interpreter is the rectory of
St. John Baptist at Bedford, where Gifford stabilized
Bunyan's conversion.

The Palace Beautiful is a mixture of Elstow Place,
the house of the Hillersdons—Renascence architecture
contrasting with the Gothic of the near church—and
Houghton Conquest, a complicated and ornate building, which would impress a village lad as immensely
magnificent, with its pillars and balconies and pedi-
ments, its curving roof-line from the front, its four
towers with their shooting double-pointed tops.
There would certainly have been arbours in its garden.
(One of the next century is extant.) And in the
account of the Pilgrim approaching along a narrow
passage leading to the porter's lodge, past two lions,
we see a tinker's memory. Bunyan must have gone
at some time, either as a boy with his father or later
by himself, to do some mending-job at the great
House. He would of course go to the porter's
lodge on the eastern side ; and the barking of the
watchdogs frightened him. In the allegory the porter
appears to bid the Pilgrim have no fear.

The Valley of the Shadow of Death we may place
near Shillbrook Village. The country round Bedford
in uniformly flat ; but here there is a sudden ravine.
The road grows narrow, with deep clefts on either
side. For a tinker used to the surrounding flat

fields, the ravine would look very menacing and impressive in the dusk. Especially if amid the gloom of the massed trees he caught a glimpse of the sparks and smoke of the blacksmith's forge and heard the echoing clang.

Vanity Fair seems a composite picture of the small Elstow Fair, which must have glamoured his childhood, and the vast Stowbridge Fair, which he probably visited in the course of his work. His description of Vanity Fair is too like the fact of Stowbridge Fair for the resemblance to be accidental. Stowbridge Fair was an important commercial event, attended by French mercers and Flemish wool-merchants as well as by traders from all over England. It was specially used for the display of novelties. There were rows and rows of booths, with areas allotted to the different trade-sections : Duddery, Ironmongers Row, Garlick Row, and so on. It had its own Court of Justice, presided over by the mayor or his deputy, who was attended by eight Redcoats. Possibly Bunyan had seen some thief or brawler arrested and tried : which gave him the idea of having Faithful tried at Vanity Fair.

The Hill called Lucre, with its rotten ground and its silver mine, was the village of Pulloxhill on its hilltop. There had once been a hope of finding gold there, and pits had been dug ; but it was yellow talc, not gold, that was found. The locality is still called Gold Close.

The Riverside seems the valley of the little river Flit.

Doubting Castle derived from the effect on the

brooding tinker of the big tree-shaded mound of Cainhoe Castle.

The Delectable Mountains are the Chilterns, which glimmered across the summer-haze as the hills from which help cometh, when the tinker plodded about in south Bedfordshire. As he moved round the country-side, they took various shapes for him, bare shoulders against the blue, or dark heaps of pine, but they always remained as a mysterious land promising a life different from that of the Bedfordshire fields of toil.

The hell-mouth, rumbling with fire and brimstone in the side of a hill, suggests the pits near the Icknield Way, once pit-dwellings. Here also were old work-ings, ancient earthwork circles, and the rumble of quarrymen at work in the great chalk-pits. As the lime was burnt on the spot, the smell is also explained.

The Enchanted Ground is perhaps the valleys in the Chilterns near Barton-le-Clay. But it is also made up, of course, of all Bunyan's pleasant memories of flower and spring and orchard. Bunyan's deep love for natural beauty is exemplified by the following two quotations :

Here he would lie down, embrace the ground, and kiss the very flowers that grew in the valley. He would now be up every morning by break of day, tracing and walking to and fro in this valley. (*Pilgrim's Progress*, II.)

Never was fair weather after foul, nor warm weather after cold, nor sweet and beautiful spring after a heavy and nipping and terrible winter, so comfortable, sweet, desirable, and welcome to the poor birds and beasts of the field as this day will be to the Church of God. Then will all the spiders and dragons and owls and foul spirits of Antichrist be

brought to light, and all the pretty robins and little birds
in the Lord's field most sweetly send forth their pleasant
notes, and all the flowers and herbs of his garden spring.
(*Holy City.*)

Note in these passages also that there is no sign
whatever of Biblical style, either in diction or rhythm.
The style of the English translation of the Bible is
majestic, hieratic, sterile. It never represented a
living speech, and therefore it never entered into
living speech. Phrases, rhythms, incantations from
it had a powerful effect on men ; but the hieratic
nature of the style, its sterile grandeur, prevented any
real fusion with language. Probably in large part
the stiffness of style came from the fact that it was the
work of men who were trying hard to translate a book
they conceived to hold the voice of the Almighty—
so that they communicated a kind of chanting
rigidity with a peculiar charm, but denying all the
shape and colour of common speech. The way that
this strange tension crept into the English version,
and seems absent from versions in other languages, is
a tribute to the poetic richness stirring in sixteenth-
century English ; but the result was an abstraction
from that richness. The Bible-idiom took its decisive shape from Tyndale, at a time when Tudor
English was stirring with its first vitalities.

If ever a writer should show the influence of the
Bible's style, he should be Bunyan ; for Bunyan must
have known the Bible almost by heart, and he had
absorbed it during years when he read scarcely any
other books. Yet all the passages which give
personal quality to his writing are derived directly

from the common speech of the day, and have nothing biblical about them. Where his style is great is in the power he has to use a concentrated form of popular idiom and rhythm.

Take the following, an ordinary passage of narrative, which shows the new simplicity that he introduced ; the way that the rise and fall of the rhythm echoes the emotional sense :

Wherefore, methought I saw Christiana and Mercy, and the boys, go all of them up to the gate : to which when they were come, they betook themselves to a short debate, about how they must manage their calling at the gate, and what should be said unto him that did open to them : so it was concluded, since Christiana was the eldest, that she should knock for entrance, and that she should speak to them that did open, for the rest. So Christiana began to knock, and, as her poor husband did, she knocked and knocked again. But instead of any that answered, they all thought that they heard as if a dog came barking upon them ; a dog, and a great one too : and this made the women and children afraid. Nor durst they for a while knock any more, for fear the mastiff should fly upon them. Now, therefore, they were greatly tumbled up and down in their minds, and knew not what to do. Knock they durst not, for fear of the dog ; go back they durst not, for fear the keeper of the gate should espy them as they so went, and should be offended with them. At last, they thought of knocking again, and knocked more vehemently than they did at first. Then said the keeper of the gate, ' Who is there ? ' So the dog left off to bark, and he opened unto them.

We may say that Bunyan has here founded the English novel. We find brilliant improvisations of every kind among the Elizabethans, rich suggestions and diversities of tone. We find, in short, everything except what we find in this passage of Bunyan's : a sensitive objectivity capable of all effects, from those of the simplest incident to those of extreme dramatic tension.

It is a token of the greatness in Bunyan that he innovated in two diametrically opposed forms : *Grace Abounding*, which is the first personal testament in English in which the pattern of an inner conflict is defined with scrupulous truth and unslackening grip ; *The Pilgrim's Progress*, which is the first book of clean-cut and objectively defined imaginative story-telling.

It is an example of the way diverse social forces intertwine, that while Bunyan was creating this style of direct narrative, the Royal Society was requiring that prose should become plain, unlaboured, simple. The needs of the passionate seeker and of the earnest scientist coincide. And the reason why they coincide is that they both derive from a triumphant class-movement determined to advance productivity and master nature. For we must not forget that Bunyan's achievement of Grace meant an acceptance of things as they were—together with the intuition of unity that represented the future. Therefore, socially divided as they were, deeply separated in ideology, he and the scientist were making up a whole.[1]

[1] Bishop Sprat says members of the Royal Society were expected to use a simple style ' bringing all things as near the mathematical plainness as they can : and preferring the language of artisans, countrymen, and merchants before those of wits and scholars '. Note what was said earlier about Bunyan's repudiation of Universities.

20

Allegory

BUT though we have seen in *The Pilgrim's Progress* the origin of the great bourgeois novel-tradition, the story is an allegory, not a novel. It stands with the other basic fantasies of world-literature : *Don Quixote, The Odyssey, The Golden Ass, Gulliver, Gargantua*. What is the common factor? The creative allegory uses a highly generalized form to cover a width of historical content which is felt to burst the bounds of any more naturalistic method. It will be noted that all the examples given are like Bunyan's book in that they deal with wanderings. They depict life as a series of trials and conflicts, from which the hero at last emerges victorious. In the work of Rabelais and Swift this structure is somewhat confused and subject to strain for reasons which there is no space here to argue out. But we may note that the prime images of Rabelais are the Giants and the irrepressible rascal of a mannikin Panurge (the ' all-maker ', man as the force who has faced the universe and means to conquer it ; but also man as the bourgeois scoundrel) ; and that these images are repeated, in direct and in inverted form, by the first two adventures of Gulliver.

Now, as it is important for the purposes of this book to get rid of any idea of ' eternal verities ' and

to show the social relation of all human thinking, we
shall deal rapidly with the problem of continuity in
expression.

During all the period we know in any form as
history man has been physically stable ; his mutations
have gone into tool and idea. So there are certain
physical experiences common to men of the various
periods. These are as follows : All men are born and
die ; they must eat, drink, excrete, and sleep ; they
must breathe ; if they live a normal length of years,
they feel the impulses of sex, mate, and beget children.
But these experiences do not exist in a void ; they are
related to an evolving social whole ; the consciousness
of them is at every point the product of social
experience. Still, there are certain common factors
that we can enumerate and define.

The birth-memory—a memory of the whole organism—gives the basic act-pattern. Rhythmic movement directed towards an end. Pain and release.
Passage from darkness to light. The cloven impulse
that hesitates between the desire to retreat and the
desire to advance. The emotion of being utterly out
of time, out of rhythm, subjected to uncontrollable
pressures ; the emotion of being perfectly in time,
in rhythm, controlling the movement of things. The
wish to arrest ; the wish to merge with the reality of
flow.

Also, the intensity of sensation in which heat and
cold, pain and bliss, exist simultaneously and
alternately.

Next, breathing : the taking in and letting out of
air. This activity strengthens the images of exit and

entrance, putting in and taking out, rhythmic movement, as the basis of life.

Next, eating and digestion. As the means whereby the baby first grapples with environment, these activities are of prime importance. Again, the putting in and taking-out pattern ; the variation of blissful fullness and colic-pang.

Sleeping and waking also become emblems of the two elements that continually conflict and merge in man to make up his wholeness.

The side of release goes ahead with the task of understanding and mastering the world. The side of bafflement and pain retreats into fear and fantasies of escape. It centres round the idea that there is a lost-self, which, being lost, must be the real-self. Emotionally, it links up with all the unconscious patterns of fear and loss. Thus it finds its chief image in birth imagined as excretion. The divided self is imagined as having voided its reality, its true-self ; and loss is felt to involve ' pollution '.

Among savages this fantasy expresses itself in the varied ideas about the external-soul. As society grows more complex, the forms taken by the notion that the true-self is lost grow more complex also. The body is the ' unreal ' self. The soul is the reality. The body is a substitute for the self lost at birth ; therefore one can be redeemed in turn by somebody or something else that takes one's place.

It will be seen, then, that we cannot treat even these ' basic forms of sense ' without admitting the historical element and showing how the forms change with the social consciousness that encloses them. It is the increase of class-division that deepens the personal conflict.

But this analysis has left out the release side. The movement of society is increasing the human mastery of Nature. So the sense of division is bound up with an increasing sense of unity and power.

There, briefly put, has been the whole of spiritual conflict in history as we know it. For history—the period from the discovery of agriculture up to our own day—has always involved class conflict and has always been patriarchal in some degree. Hence the way that there is a certain uniformity in its idioms of growth and recoil. But what is equally significant is the new element that each stage of history adds to the ' basic forms '.

We cannot imagine humanity outgrowing those basic forms—that is, ceasing to be born and die, eat and excrete, breathe and sleep. Thus it is of particular interest to see these forms as they appear at each decisive historical stage. From the days of the myths of early Egypt and Babylonia up to the great allegories which we have mentioned, there are certain important similarities.

The tale of the wandering soul appears fully blown in the myths of Osiris, Herakles, Gilgamesh, and the like. To understand the form that the tale here takes we must realize that astronomy was the science that most enabled men to get a grip on the universe in those early days ; it was bound up with all their productive methods. The passage of the sun through the Zodiac became the chief image for victorious movement. Herakles with his Twelve Labours is the sun passing through the Twelve Signs of the Zodiac, each sign being imagined as a trial or conflict. The Egyptians developed a highly complicated account of the sun's passage through the twelve hours of the night in the under-earth, each hour involving a terrible danger. The story of Odysseus passing through his various trials seems to be a rationalized version of Phoenician myth telling of the Voyages of Ishtar through the Seven Gates of the West to the Land of the Dead. Seven is a lunar number, as twelve is solar.

When we come to the imagery of the tests themselves in these myths, we find that the predominating image is that of birth as a violent battle. And as this birth-image is always confused with the images of digestion, the commonest form of fear is the fear of being eaten alive. Usually the cannibal is a giant—that is, the huge parental form as remembered through the haze of infantile sense-impressions and thought-processes. The folklore of England, as of other countries, is full of stories of giants and cannibals ; and Bunyan would certainly have heard such stories as a child. But unless they drew charges of meaning from his unconscious store of infantile memories, seeming to corroborate his experience, they would not exert any power or lurk in his mind, to reappear in *The Pilgrim's Progress*.

The astronomical formulation is imposed on the great basic myth-form emerging from the agricultural struggle. In that myth-form the images of the birth-trauma are evoked, in order that their defeat may be chronicled and represented. The personal

181

birth-struggle is projected upon the struggle with the seasonal earth. The Old and the Young Year battle for the possession of the Mother Earth. The Old Man of Winter, the Dying Year, is defeated by the Young Year of growth and spring-energy. Spring and autumn, renewal and fertility, are the two points of rest, of triumph ; tragedy and comedy are born.

We find, then, all the great allegories, like myths, show many common forms grouped round birth-imagery, however different is the enveloping social content. To take instances from each allegory mentioned : in the *Odyssey* we have the Sirens who eat the drowned sailors, the cannibal-mother ; or the giant Cyclops in his cave, the cannibal-father ; or Scylla with her devouring animal-loins. In the *Golden Ass*, the hero is changed into an ass, a ' dumb beast ' who, like the baby that cannot speak, is subjected to all kinds of trials and miseries while he is advancing towards initiation into the meaning of life. In *Gargantua*, the giant-fantasies are directly liberated as well as birth-imageries. In *Don Quixote*, the hero, like Lucius of the *Golden Ass*, goes wandering through ceaseless indignities and drubbings in search of meaning in an incomprehensible world. In *Gulliver*, we have first the giant-fantasy in two forms ; and then, in a fierce recoil against capitalist values (which are taken for human values), we get the glorification of the innocent dumb beast as against the actual world of adult activity.

Bunyan's work is directly in the line of great allegory, and therefore closely related to the central

European myths. Like Herakles or Osiris, his Pilgrim passes through his manifold labours, his crises of trial. It is no doubt accidental that, like these other emblems of the sun, he has twelve places of transition and struggle : the Slough, the House of the Interpreter, the Cross, the Hill of Difficulty, the Valley of Humiliation and the Valley of the Shadow, Vanity Fair, Doubting Castle, Delectable Mountains, Enchanted Ground, Beulah, and the City of Light. But his progress is certainly developed out of folk-intuitions very similar to those from which the sun-progresses were conceived.

The pictures on the walls of the Interpreter's House have much the same meaning as the pictures on the walls of an Egyptian tomb. They are meant to guide the 'wandering soul'. (Sometimes Bunyan's symbolic diction becomes very Egyptian, as in this sentence from *The Holy War*, ' The King and his Son being *All*, and always *Eye*, could not but discern all passages in his dominion '. That suggests strongly Ra and Hor, the Father and the Uadjit.) Indeed, Bunyan's description of the Wanderings of the Pilgrim is directly in the key of the ancient mystery-conceptions.

The passage from darkness to light is a predominating image ; and that, as we have noted, is one of the basic ideas of significant movement developed out of the birth-memory. The battle with the monster in the earth-cleft is the common folk-image of the birth-struggle. A monster such as Apollyon has the same meaning as, say, the Minotaur whom Theseus slays after tracking down the lair through the wandering maze, or Cacus whom Hercules tracks down to his den. These monsters are male, the destroying Father in his ugliest shape. The Pilgrim's imprisonment by a giant, and his escape from the dark cell, are paralleled by countless tales in folklore and myth, of which that of Ulysses in the Cyclops' cave, or that of Jack the Giant-killer, will serve as examples. The crossing of the Slough or of the River belongs to the commonest type of birth-symbolism. The ceaseless sound of ' many waters ' pervading the bridge-jail would help in arousing birth-memories in Bunyan. ' This River ', says Mr. Standfast, ' has been a terror to me, yea the thoughts of it also have often frighted me. But now, methinks, I stand easy, my foot is fixed upon that which the feet of the priests that bear the covenant stood while Israel went over this Jordan '. Remember the way that the fear-side of Bunyan's birth-memory had always much concerned itself with the image of drowning, and we can realize that as he lay in the bridge-jail and listened to the waters, he must have felt afraid they would sap the foundations and bring him down in a crash of masonry. For only a short while previously, in 1673–4, the bridge-dungeon had actually been carried away by a flooding of the river ; the entry in the Corporation Records says, ' Through a sudden inundation of the Ouse the stone house called the Bridge House in this town is partially fallen down and the rest much shaken and like to fall, and the foundation or pile whereon it stood, a great part washed away '. Not till 1675 was the bridge-prison reconstructed. Since Bunyan spent the winter and spring of 1675–6 in this prison, he would know that he was living in a building which had not been tested against the winter and spring floods, and he might well listen attentively to the waters, until the image of passing over the River to safety became strongly fixed in his mind, as an image of consummation. In 1688 he published a book, *The Water of Life*, in which the river-symbol is elaborately expounded.

The lions menacing in the narrow way are again symbols of the difficult birth-egress. Scylla with the ravening loin-beasts we have mentioned. An instance from nearer home—from the Dane Hills of Leicestershire—is Black Annis, a giant ogress who lived on the flesh of lambs and children, who had ' vast talons foul with human flesh ', and whose ' obscene waist, warm skins of human victims close embraced '. Here is the female ogre, the Mother in her ugliest shape.

Slay-good, the giant in the second part of the *Progress*, is an ogre. ' The giant was rifling of him, with a purpose, after that, to pick his bones ; for he was of the nature of flesh-eaters '. And, like the Cyclops or Black Annis and most of his fellows, he lives in a cave—a recess in mother-earth.

We may note that the image of the Devourer is the basic one used by all the protesters against the Enclosures in England. Cormorants, greedy gulls, men that would eat up men, women, and children, are the phrases that Crowley quotes as in common use among the people. Caterpillars and locusts were other terms in general use. The idiom persists. Two centuries later Clare talks of vile unsatiated maws that devour the birthright of the poor. This image of the oppressors as cannibals links up with the deep-

rooted folk-images we are considering. Slay-good is
' master of a number of thieves ' as well as an ogre.
Diabolus in *The Holy War* is a ' mighty giant ', and
the call to the citizens of Mansoul is to throw off
' the slavery of the giant '.

The dropping of the burden at the foot of the Cross
brings us to the traditional Christian images, which
Bunyan was merely using in the accepted way. But
to complete our analysis, we had better touch on the
general meanings. When the burden drops, the
division of the self is ended ; the external-soul,
the lost-self, the other-self. Redemption ends the
division. By losing your soul, you find it. But the
burden is also the weight of the oppressors that
the poor man carried on his back. It is the Old Man,
the devil-father, sitting on him like the Old Man
of the Sea with the strangle-grip on Sinbad ; and for
Bunyan it is specifically the tinker's wallet which
marked him out as a despised toiler as he trudged
the roads. The dropping of the burden that results
from the conviction of grace is thus the intuition of
the social unity that will some day result from the
throwing off of the parasite. The Cross originally
was the symbol of immortality, being a schematic
representation of the mated loins ; as the Ankh it
stood for the unceasing flow of race-life. But as the
sense of division increased, the birth-image was no
longer one of release, of forward movement. It
expressed only obstruction and pang. It was
imagined now with the child torn to pieces and fixed
hopelessly upon it.

While dealing with Bunyan's allegorical figures, we

may point out that the Man with the Muckrake is not a symbol of pruriency, as he is usually taken to be. He represents the blindly-accumulating capitalist, who cannot see the offered crown of grace. What he is raking together are ' straws and sticks and the dust of the floor '.

We have now traced out many elements that can be paired off with similar ones in ancient myth. Yet we cannot reduce *The Pilgrim's Progress* to any of those myths. It has an inclusive purpose, a direction, a colouring of character, a degree of tension, a structure of drama, which make it the work of one period and of no other.[1]

[1] The dumb-beast symbol has many more ramifications than are mentioned in the text here. One is its relation to the Mother, the supreme beast of burden, since she carries the child. (Note how Jesus enters the promised city on an ass.) Another important point is the worker as beast of burden. (We have seen Bunyan with his wallet as the Pilgrim with his burden.) From this point of view Swift's Houyhnhnms are the Working Class. Note how his description of ' civilized man ' to the horses is a description entirely of the upper or propertied classes! Note again how Appuleius equates the wretched beasts and the workers in his realistic description of the baker's workhouse, showing that his extension of sympathy for the dumb-beast, so poignant in parts of his allegory, includes fellow-feeling for the human toiler.

21

Dream

IF we look at the title-page of the first edition of
The Pilgrim's Progress, the word that starts out at
us is the huge DREAM. Throughout Bunyan keeps up
the fiction that he is relating a dream. The meaning
is that he is giving in symbol-form the story of his
own life, and that to follow out the inner content we
must use the method of dream-analysis. Not of
course that Bunyan thought like that. He merely
knew that what he wanted to say transcended any of
the ordinary forms at his disposal. As he gives us in
Grace Abounding one of his dreams, we can analyse
that to grasp his method.

About this time, the state and happiness of these poor
people at Bedford was thus, in a dream or vision, represented
to me. I saw, as if they were set on the sunny side of some
high mountain, there refreshing themselves with the
pleasant beams of the sun, while I was shivering and
shrinking in the cold, afflicted with frost, snow, and dark
clouds. Methought, also, betwixt me and them, I saw a
wall that did compass about this mountain; now, through
this wall my soul did greatly desire to pass; concluding,
that if I could, I would go even into the very midst of them,
and there also comfort myself with the heat of the sun.
About this wall I thought myself, to go again and again,

188

still prying as I went, to see if I could find some way or passage, by which I might enter therein; but none could I find for some time. At the last, I saw, as it were, a narrow gap, like a little doorway in the wall, through which I attempted to pass; but the passage being very strait and narrow, I made many efforts to get in, but all in vain, even until I was well-nigh quite beat out, by striving to get in; at last, with great striving, methought I at first did get in my head, and after that, by a sidling striving, my shoulders, and my whole body; then I was exceeding glad, and sat down in the midst of them, and so was comforted with the light and heat of the sun.

In this short account of a dream we have the whole of *The Pilgrim's Progress* compressed.

First let us take the physical imagery. It is directly of birth. He wants to make the passage from pain to bliss, from dark to light. But there is an obstruction in the way. He cannot find the easy passage. Hence the image of birth as a long, winding passage. The ritual expression of this in the past was the maze or labyrinth and the dances of interweaving figures associated with the labyrinth idea. ' Those crooked lanes that lead down to the chambers of death ' is a typical Bunyan phrase (from *The Heavenly Footman*). The minotaur who awaited the victim-lads or girls in the Cretan labyrinth was the cannibal beast-father— probably in fact a brazen figure in which they were roasted, or, like the Carthaginian Moloch, an idol on which they were placed to roll into the fire. For we must realize that these fears which we now analyse as obscure source-images of anxiety were once, in days when man was still insecure as master of the earth, the compelling emotions of his ritual.

JOHN BUNYAN

Bunyan in his dreams seeks to squeeze through the narrow uterine gap which seems determined to hold him for ever on the side of darkness, pain, and privation. He mimes the birth-process, gradually worming through the gap, as women used to pass a sick child through a holed stone or a cleft tree (under the emotion that the symbolic passing through the hole would constitute an easy, successful birth and remove the disabilities left by the maiming actuality). Such mimings are to be found everywhere in primitive ritual. For instance, the passing through the skin of the sacrificed bull or gazelle in ancient Egypt ; the rite of the Tikenou which was called ' the passing through the skin-cradle '.

In *The Pilgrim's Progress* the Pilgrim is all the while fighting his way through valleys and narrow places so that he may at last come to the final haven of light.

In all Bunyan's works we find a quantity of dilemma images that plainly use the birth-memory. For instance, he tells us that sometimes he could preach with a spontaneous flow, at other times he felt as if his ' head had been in a bag all the time '. And thus he speaks of the distracting pull of the devil against God :

I often when these temptations have been with force upon me, did compare myself in the case of such a child, whom some gypsy hath by force took up under her apron, and is carrying from friend and country ; kick sometimes I did, and also scream and cry ; but yet I was as bound in the wings of the temptation. . . .

And thus the image of birth as drowning appears to express indecision :

DREAM

I did now feel myself to sink into a gulf. . . . I did liken myself in this condition, unto the case of a child that was fallen into a mill-pit, who, though it could make some shift to scrabble and spraul in the water, yet because it could find neither hold for hand nor foot, therefore at last it must die on that condition.

(Remember that Bunyan himself was almost drowned twice.) The physical imagery of his dream is not, then, difficult to understand. But we have not touched the deeper emotional meaning.

He wants to get out of an old form of existence, as the baby at the end of its time feels compelled to move out from the womb. But because he cannot complete the passage into the new world, where life achieves a new totality of meaning, he is held in the cleft-stick of suffering and privation.

The new world that he sees but cannot join is the world of conviction he felt in the old women sunning themselves at their doors in Bedford. They had come out through the doors of time into a world where they could find entire satisfaction. He wanted to join them, but the obstructing pressures held him back.

We know what those pressures were. They were the social discords which he could not resolve ; and seeking for a basic pattern of physical life which will reflect the basic pattern of social experience, he develops this imagery of the dream. He wants to understand, to get back to origins. So the reduction of the social dilemma to the personal dilemma of birth, though failing to explain, does provide a palliative for pain that would otherwise destroy.

He wants to get outside the hampering old-body into the vivid world of light and comfort.

That world is the beckoning world of fellowship that he intuited in the Bedford group. 'Fellowship' is the word he uses himself. He understood clearly enough the general emotional import of his dream. The mountain of comforting light was ' the Church of the living God ', he said. He wanted to get outside the cramping, distorting social discord of his day into the fuller life of fellowship.

Apply this analysis to his allegory, and the allegory's meaning is transformed. The world of light is not the land of death. It is the future of fellowship. The tale tells of the passage from privation and obstruction to light and joy and plenty. The heaven-symbol is brought down from beyond-death ; it becomes a symbol of what earth could be made by fellowship.

Thus the allegory, which superficially is a story of how to die, is a stimulus to further living. Bunyan had broken through the obstruction and entered the light of fellowship that made his Bedford congregation so dear. But though that communion was infinitely precious to him, it could not fully satisfy ; for it was only a tiny section of life. The full fellowship still remained as a beckoning light, not drawing him towards death, but confirming him in his ardour of living.

Thus we show how the contradictions within the allegory resolve emotionally, though they still remain in the terms of formulation.

Bunyan was aware of the contradictions. He felt uneasy about the way that his Pilgrim had to desert his wife and children, and he introduced later in the story a discussion on the subject ; Charity upbraids Christian. But he could not overcome this discord.

Similarly, in the second part, where Christiana sets out with the children to join her husband, he cannot bear to make a holocaust of the whole family. He makes Christiana wade over the river at the end and leave her children behind. The picture is ridiculous. Here are husband and wife rushing off to death as the only consummation of their purpose, yet the children are left to wander about on the banks of the death-river before they too are allowed to get over into heaven.

Bunyan here confessed his sense that something was wrong about the idea of death as the goal of life. But while writing the tales themselves, while concerned with the struggles and trials of his characters, while emotionally accepting the light outside as an image of fuller life, a new quality of life, he overcame the contradictions. Only when he had to bring the allegory into logical line with the assumed thesis of death as fulfilment did he begin to feel uneasy and to play about with the details to obscure as much as possible the consequences of that thesis.

His dream gives the clue. It explains the underlying social basis which the story of ' personal salvation ' contradicts at every point but is quite unable to abolish. In fact, the contradiction is rooted in the whole method of the story. Literally, there is only one character—the Pilgrim. He meets phantasms of his own good and evil, and dies. He does nothing but make a lot of faces in a mirror. He is utterly

alone. Such an abstracted individual could in fact
experience nothing, for he would be only a dance of
atoms in a non-human void.

The impression conveyed by the allegory is the
exact opposite of what it literally professes. The
phantasms of good and evil become the real world ;
and in encountering them the Pilgrim lives through
the life that Bunyan had known in definite place and
time. The pattern of his experience, the fall and
the resolute rising-up, the loss and the finding, the
resistance and the overcoming, the despair and the
joy, the dark moaning valleys and the singing in the
places of the flowers—it is the pattern of Bunyan's
strenuous life. There are comrades and enemies,
stout-hearts and cravens, men who care only for the
goal of fellowship and men of greed and fear ; and
these are the men of contemporary England.

The Celestial City is the dream of all England, all
the world, united in Fellowship. Meanwhile there
was, for Bunyan, the little congregation of Bedford
who were doing their best in a world of distorting
pressures. Bunyan got through the gap to his place
of fellowship. Some day, perhaps not so very far
off, all England will throw off the distorting pressures
and make the dream of full fellowship true.

Before passing on, we will return to an important
instance in Bunyan's writings of the effects of birth-
memory. He is telling of his tricks to catch God :

I had tempted God ; and on this manner did I do it.
Upon a time my wife was great with child, and before her

full time was come, her pangs, as of a woman in travail, were fierce and strong upon her, even as if she would have immediately fallen in labour, and been delivered of an untimely birth. Now, at this very time it was that I had been so strongly tempted to question the being of God; wherefore, as my wife lay crying by me, I said, but with all secrecy imaginable, even thinking in my heart, Lord, if thou wilt now remove this sad affliction from my wife and cause that she be troubled no more therewith this night, and now were her pangs just upon her, then I shall know that thou canst discern the most secret thoughts of the heart.

I had no sooner said it in my heart, but her pangs were taken from her, and she was cast into a deep sleep. . . . So when I waked in the morning, it came upon me again, even what I had said in my heart the last night, and how the Lord had showed me that he knew my secret thoughts, which was a great astonishment unto me for several weeks after.

The prayer that the pangs should cease represented a prayer that birth should have no pangs at all; also a wish to keep the babe (as a self-projection) for ever in the womb, safe from the attacking world. The meaning of the test was: If the Father grants this prayer, he will show that birth *can* be painless, woundless, and so he will erase the wounds that serve as anxiety-centres in my own flesh. The Father will truly be the Deliverer.

We can grasp the emotion behind this episode if we compare the prayer for the pangs to cease with Bunyan's direct pleas to the Father. 'I have with many a bitter sigh cried, Good Lord, break it open; Lord, break open these gates of brass and cut these bars of iron asunder. . . .'

JOHN BUNYAN

(What tremendous powers of discipline that a man with so extreme a sense of claustrophobic birth-terror should have spent over twelve years in jail without going mad—emerging, on the contrary, with faculties vastly more sensitively coherent.)

That Bunyan felt the whole process of reconciliation with the Father as birth-mime is shown by such phrases as the following : ' Alas, alas, it is as possible for a man, when the pangs of guilt are upon him, to forbear praying, as it is for a woman, when the pangs of travail are upon her, to forbear crying '. And his images for Regeneration are uniformly those of the birth-trauma in all its violence. ' The glory of the holiness of God did at this time break me to pieces ; and the bowels and compassion of Christ did break me as on the wheel ; for I could not consider him but as a lost and rejected Christ, the remembrance of which was as the continual breaking of my bones.' ' I was as if my loins were broken, or as if my hands and feet had been tied and bound with chains.' ' That I might for ever be inflamed with the sight, and joy, and communion with him whose head was crowned with thorns, whose face was spit on, and body broken, and soul made an offering for my sins. . . . I lay continually trembling at the mouth of hell.' ' Grace was in all thy tears, grace came bubbling out of thy side with thy blood. . . . Grace came out where the whip smote thee, where the nails and spear pierced thee.' Traditional images, but uttered with all the freshness of personal experience.

And the travelling Pilgrims are spelt in his allegory ' travailers '.

22

Thrift

WHEN released again from prison, Bunyan completed *The Pilgrim's Progress* and went on with
his work as pastor. In his attempts to devise a
Christian morality—that is, a morality for the petty-
bourgeois at this particular moment of capitalist
transition—we find the more compromising side of
his sense of grace. The conviction of reconciliation
with the Father had enabled him to find the point of
equilibrium from which he could build his *Grace
Abounding* and *Pilgrim's Progress* : his conflict defined
from the subjective and from the objective angles.
At the same time it had necessitated an acceptance of
the moment of historical process in which he found
himself. As part of that acceptance he identified
himself with the dissenting petty-bourgeois and
labourers, the restlessly active class from whom the
great industrial movement of the next century was to
come.

In writings like *Christian Behaviour . . . teaching
Husbands, Wives, Parents, Children, Masters, Servants, &c.
how to walk so as to please God* (1663), he had done his
part in moralizing the class-needs of the petty-
bourgeois. What was the first principle of ethics of

this class, which was chafing against the restrictions on trade and industry? It was thrift.

Throughout the Protestant movements we find that the question of thrift is a root-question. From Wiclif on, the middle-class anger against the Church is based always on anger at the Church's parasitism, the maintenance of a vast unproductive organization, and the diversion of moneys into the Church's coffers instead of into trade and industry. Even movements, such as that of the Franciscans, which went on inside the Church—since at their period capitalism was too immature to attempt successfully a secession—are emotionally based on the principles that led to Protestantism when feudalism was further decayed. St. Francis said to a lazy brother, ' Fly, Brother, since thou art minded to eat up the labour of thy Brothers and to be idle in God's work as a drone that winneth nothing nor worketh, but eateth up the work and labour of the good bees '. In that speech, recorded by Brother Leo, we see the whole basis of Protestantism in embryo.

Thrift was needed as part of the process of accumulation whereby industry was speeded on its course. Thrift alone would never have created industrialism. The social dynamic came from the seizure of the land by the upper classes ; but the thrift of the lower middle classes was also necessary. It provided the ceaseless little petty-bourgeois centres of activity from which industrialism stemmed.

Hence the way that the loose-liver, the debauchee, became the figure of evil. Recall the horror that came over Bunyan about dancing. It seems a long way from that such a wildly idiosyncratic terror to an ethic of thrift based on class-needs ; yet the connexion is there. William Prynne, typical Puritan moralist, clinched his condemnation of dancing with the statement : ' They that work hard all day had more need to rest than to dance all night. And yet how many there are who after a hard journey or toilsome day's work will take more pains at night in dancing than they did in labouring all the daytime.' It is the same pressure of social instability, gradually creating a class-ethic, which revealed itself in the dogmatist's denunciation and the village-lad's dark fear. We must also remember that the games— maypoles and wakes and so on—were bound up with a general medieval viewpoint based on magic ; so that the Puritans were not merely ousting innocent enjoyment, they were concerned primarily with ' idolatry ', the primitive magical ideas imbedded in the revelries. Yet the revolt against magic and the ethic of thrift merge inseparably in the needs of the progressive classes. The puritan fight against jun-keting saints' days combined the thrift-urge with this horror of all cultural activities that had magical associations.

The following passage from a letter by John Wall in 1659 to Milton is illuminating. It shows the spearhead of social consciousness at that date. Wall realizes that why the Commonwealth regime is failing is because the economic development of England is not yet mature enough to carry an effective democracy ; that the first need is economic progress, which will inevitably bring in its train the basis of a securer freedom :

You complain of the non-proficiency of the nation, and of its retrogade motion of late, in liberty and spiritual truths. It is much to be bewailed ; but yet let us pity human frailty. When those who made deep protestations of their zeal for our liberty both spiritual and civil, and made the fairest offers to be assertors thereof, and whom we thereupon trusted ; when those, being instated in power, shall betray the good thing committed to them, and lead us back to Egypt, and by that force which we gave them to win us liberty hold us fast in chains ; what can we poor people do ? You know who they were that watched our Saviour's sepulchre to keep him from rising.

Besides, whilst people are not free, but straightened in accommodations for life, their spirits will be dejected and servile : and conducing to that end, there should be an improving of our native commodities, as our manufactures, our fishery, our fens, forests, and commons, and our trade at sea, &c. which would give the body of the nation a comfortable subsistence ; and the breaking that cursed yoke of tithes would much help thereto.

This letter is of the greatest importance. In it we see consciously and rationally stated what was only a class-emotion in Prynne and Bunyan. (The watchers who keep the body of the son-of-man from rising are the soldiers, the rule of force resulting from property. In the words of the contemporary theorist Harrington, ' If the property of the nobility be the pastures of that beast (the army), the ox knows his master's crib '. Property is a form of force.)

Note three things in Wall's letter : the sense of

betrayal, which is what we have analysed at length in Bunyan's agony over the selling of the birthright ; the awareness that liberty can only be actualized by a lift in the productive mechanism, which is what appears in the petty-bourgeois ethic of thrift ; the sense that feudalism has still strong roots of parasitism while an established Church exists, which was throughout a slogan rallying the dissenters.[1]

Thus the sense of betrayal and the need to rush on with the economic task coalesced to produce the Nonconformist ethic which was to guide in the next century the petty-bourgeois industrialists and inventors of Cornwall, Lancashire, Scotland. It was already clearly recognized by the advanced thinkers of the age that it was the dissenters who were the basis of economic development. In William Petty's *Political Arithmetic*, 1690, we find the generalization firmly stated, ' The trade of any country is chiefly managed by the Heterodox party '. Therefore toleration is absolutely necessary if there is to be economic prosperity. ' For the Advancement of Trade, if that be a sufficient reason, indulgence must be granted in Matters of Opinion.' Here was the convincing argument for freedom, on which the advance of the next two centuries was built.

Two passages by the shrewd Petty are of especial interest :

It being natural for men to differ in opinion in matters

---

[1] For instance : The Husbandman's Plea against Tithes : Two Petitions . . . by divers Freemen of Hertford, 1647. ' The husbandman's labour is envied him, and others, by a State policy, live upon his labour.' Throughout Fox's *Journal* we see the paid priest as the emblem of all that is unrighteous in society.

above sense and reason, and for those who have less Wealth, to think they have more Wit and Understanding, especially of the things of God, which they think chiefly belong to the poor. . . .

Dissenters . . . are, for the most part, thinking, sober and patient men, and such as believe that their labour and industry is their duty towards God : how erroneous soever their opinions be. These people, believing in the Justice of God, and seeing the most licentious persons to enjoy most of the world and its best things, will never venture to be of the same religion and profession with voluptuaries and men of extreme wealth and power, whom they think to have their portion in this world.[1]

The thrift of the dissenters, laying up treasure in heaven, was laying the basis of a new world ; and the loose-liver became the symbol of all that impeded, all that was reactionary and feudalist. Note how Baxter coupled together Gentlemen and Beggars and Servile Tenants as the ' strength of iniquity '.

So Bunyan, as a prophet of the fellowship of the future, did his part in creating class-discipline. We have already noted typical instances of rebuke for wanton ways. We see the equally typical determination to maintain the ethic of thrift when we find the Church deciding that ' some days be set apart for humiliation with fasting and prayer to God because

[1] Typical statements in this relation by Bunyan are : ' It may be the servants of some men, as the horse-keeper, ploughman, scullion, etc. are more looking after heaven than their masters '. Looking after heaven means surely : advancing the doctrine of godly thrift. ' I am apt to think sometimes that more servants than masters, that more tenants than landlords, will inherit the kingdom of heaven.' (*The Heavenly Footman.*) ' Why should he (Christ) so easily take a denial of the great ones that were the grandeur of the world, and struggle so hard for hedge-creepers and highwaymen ? ' (*The Jerusalem Sinner.*)

of some disorders arising among the congregation
specially for that some have run into debt more than
they can satisfy, to the great dishonour and scandal of
religion '. When a member was found ' negligent
and unfaithful as to the management of his sister's
employment, which he was entrusted with ', and also
' contracting many debts which he neither was able
to pay, neither did he honestly and Christianly take
care to pay his creditors in due time as he ought,
though he had been often exhorted to it and admonished before by his brethren,' he had communion withdrawn from him.

In 1680 Bunyan published *The Life and Death of Mr.
Badman*, in which he realistically described the
Enemy. But, as we have seen that Grace meant for
Bunyan both an acceptance of the present and an
intuition of the future, so the Enemy is seen as a
mixture of the profligate and the rascally business-
man. His rascalities are conceived as expressions of a
lack of self-control that makes him in the end an
unreliable and unstable member of his class. Thus
Bunyan is simultaneously developing the ethic on
which capitalism was brought into full swing, and
denouncing the types of greed which capitalism could
not but encourage. Both his sense of unity and his
creed of class-discipline (which was to come to fulfilment in the ironmasters, Quaker bankers, inventors,
and so on, of the eighteenth century) repudiate the
parasitic types which were to predominate as capitalist
once finance-capital finally succeeded in dominating
industry in the nineteenth century. His book thus,
in championing the early creative industrialist against

the parasitic capitalist, shows the contradiction involved by capitalism from the start, though it could become destructive of the system only when a certain degree of development had been reached.

Here, then, is Bunyan's picture of the Enemy, which is also a minutely realistic picture of the wicked capitalist at this early stage. Probably the wrath of the book is partly derived from the fact that in 1680 there had been a fight between Bunyan and one John Wildman, a member of the church, who was ' extraordinarily guilty of a kind of raillery and very great passion ', and who accused Bunyan of making privy inquiries among the women to find out how high he could estimate the church-levy to come from their menfolk.

23

Mr. Badman

MR. BADMAN was an inventor of bad words, the ringleader and master sinner from a child, although his parents were in no way ungodly. He was a great liar ; and he used to pilfer. When his father spoke to him, he hung his head in a sullen manner, and grumbled and muttered his replies. Egged on by his companions, he robbed orchard and fowlhouse, and talked and laughed about his exploits afterwards. He hated going to church, and slept or whispered during the service. He gloried in cursing and swearing.

His father made him an apprentice to a friend who was an honest tradesman. Badman, however, continued to degenerate. He read books of bawdry and romance. At church now, if he did not sleep, he ogled a girl. After a year and a half of prentice-work, he became friendly with three other wicked lads, one a boozer, one a thief, one a lecher. (Giving the reasons why drink is bad, Bunyan begins, ' It greatly tendeth to impoverish and beggar a man '.)

Badman ran off from his master once or twice ; so the next time the master let him go. Badman now joined a master to his liking, neglected his work, whored, and tried to seduce the daughters of the house. His master cursed him in his own vein, and then afterwards would joke about his misdoings. Badman was said to have a bastard about this time.

When his time was done, he went to his father. He acted a modest part for a while, wanting money to set himself up. His father gave him the money, but he speedily ran into debt and was only saved from collapse by the suggestion that he would marry a rich wife. His failure resulted chiefly from his readiness to be jack-pay-for-all at the alehouse and to lend money to his fellow debauchees, who knew how to flatter him.

At last, after about two years and a half, he decided to marry. He played the godly part and won a young orphaned heiress, who, deluded by his wiles, forgot to ask the advice of a sound preacher (such as Mr. John Bunyan). But as soon as he was married, he threw off the mask and took to heavy drinking and whoring again, and tried to suppress his wife's religion and prevent her from going to sermons. To cow her, he threatened to harry her co-religionists as an informer.

He had now settled his old debts with his wife's money and set up a large shop, where he ran into worse debt than ever, and became a fraudulent bankrupt. By selling under cost, he drove a big trade, seemed to be prospering, and thus obtained credit up to four to five thousand pounds. Then he wrote a wily letter to his creditors about his misfortunes and his desire to pay to the best of his abilities, and he sent a confederate round to negotiate the terms. After

long arguments in which taxes, bad debts, badness of
the times, were blamed, he offered two and sixpence
in the pound, raising it later to five shillings on the
outcry of the creditors. And with that he got away,
some thousands the better for the transaction.

(Bunyan has a very strict passage on the ethics of
bankruptcy. The bankrupt must not only offer all
he has, except what is needed to keep his family
alive ; he must be ready to go to jail or to be at his
creditors' service ' till by labour and travail he hath
made them such amends . . . for the wrong that he
hath done them '.)

Badman continued with his cheats, overcharging,
mixing bad goods with better, denying that payments
had been made unless witnesses had been by, taking
advantage of any scarcity, which was the grave sin of
extortion. (Bunyan violently attacks all who take
advantage of the poor in any way ; for instance, by
overcharging for goods that they know the poor cannot trudge all the way to market to buy. In this
instance we see how the middleman was breaking up
the direct market-exchange. Bunyan further attacks
usury, or the taking of interest on money, where
food-commodities are involved. Pawnbrokers he
abominates. ' Those vile wretches called pawnbrokers, that lend money and goods to poor people,
who are by necessity forced to such inconvenience ',
charging £50 a year interest at times, and grabbing the
pawned objects by some cheat. He denounces any
deal in which profit is gained at somebody else's
expense, ignorant that *all* profit can only be at
somebody's expense. He tries to formulate laws of

equitable dealing, reverting to the medieval notion of
a just price : a notion possible only in a static community. This century of Bunyan's was showing how
untenable it was, with capitalist methods forcing up
the cost of living ; but Bunyan still clung to the
ideas of the early Protestants with regard to finance.
In this repudiation of the financial side of capitalism
we see the characteristic idiom of the productive
petty-bourgeois.)

Badman now grew very overweening, and at the
same time his surly side grew stronger. One night
he was thrown by his horse when coming home from
an alehouse, and broke his leg. While lying sick,
he became frightened and swore reform ; and he
was very tender to his wife. But, recovering, he
turned his old self again ; and this broke her heart.
She died. There were some children by this marriage,
who were weak mixtures of the parents, superficially
respectable, but underneath corrupt.

After his wife's death, Badman did not marry again.
When asked why, he answered, 'Who would keep a
cow of his own that can have a quart of milk for a
penny?' But he became entangled with an alehouse
whore, finally brought her home, and lived a cat-and-
dog life with her. They stayed together some sixteen
to seventeen years, and then parted poor as owlets,
having worn each other out. Badman became drop-
sical, and was said to have 'a tang of the pox in his
bowels'. Though not an old man, he mouldered
away. This time, however, he maintained his equa-
nimity, talking only business, gossip, or politics with

his visitors, and at last died as quietly as a lamb or a chrisom-child.

That, in brief, is the story of Mr. Badman ; and even this bald summary shows that once again Bunyan had pioneered with a literary form that was to have a fruitful future. What, however, prevents the book from being a masterpiece worthy to set beside the autobiography and the allegory is that the narrative is interspersed with long moralizings.

But if one subtracts the moralizings, one finds that here is the first realistic novel. One makes this claim without forgetting the work that Elizabethans such as Deloney had done. Bunyan's tale is the first imaginative reconstruction of a character-type drawn directly from experience, a coherent definition of an individual within his social area—the progress of that individual being shown by a steady narrative, and the psychological reactions of each stage in the progress being grasped with masterly insight.

Here, in short, are all the elements of the classic bourgeois novel. Defoe, Bunyan's dissenting successor in the next generation, built directly on this method of Bunyan's, merely omitting the tedious moral digressions.

The work is of course openly a propaganda-lesson. Yet with what æsthetic self-control does Bunyan tell the tale. The peaceful deathbed of Badman, for instance. Once he is launched on the tale, Bunyan's feeling for honest character-drawing directs the whole construction. He gives Badman just the traits of good-humour that are needed to round out his character with full conviction. And he has many a side-light of incisive humour or satire. Thus he tells about the woman whom Badman brought home after his wife's death :

She had her companions as well as he had his, and she would meet them too at the tavern and alehouse more commonly than he was aware of. To be plain, she was a very whore, and had as great resort come to her, where time and place was appointed, as any of them all. Aye, and he smelt it too, but could not tell how to help it. For if he began to talk, she could lay in his dish the whores that she knew he haunted, and she could fit him also with cursing and swearing, for she would give him oath for oath, and curse for curse.

And as a specimen of the narrative we may quote the following :

It was but a little while after he was married, but he hangs his religion upon the hedge, or rather dealt with it as men deal with their old clothes, who cast them off, or leave them to others to wear; for his part he would be religious no longer.

Now therefore he had pulled off his vizard, and began to show himself in his old shape, a base, wicked, debauched fellow; and now the poor woman saw that she was betrayed indeed, now also his old companions began to flock about him and to haunt the house and shop as formerly. And who with them but Mr. Badman? And who with him again but they?

Now those good people that used to company with his wife began to be amazed and discouraged, also he would frown and glout upon them as if he abhorred the appearance of them, so that in little time he drove all good company from her, and made her sit solitary by herself. He also began now to go out a-nights to those drabs who were his familiars before, with whom he would stay sometimes till midnight, and sometimes till almost morning, and then would come home as drunk as a swine : and this was the course of Mr. Badman.

Now when he came home in this case, if his wife did but speak a word to him about where he had been and why he had so abused himself, though her words were spoken in never so much meekness and love, then she was whore, and bitch, and jade ! and it was well if she missed his fingers and heels. Sometimes also he would bring his punks home to his house, and woe be to his wife when they were gone if she did not entertain them with all varieties possible, and also carry it lovingly to them.

Here, in compressed but unmistakable form, is the method of the great bourgeois novel. The confused or romantic focus that rules in Elizabethan fiction is ended. A coherent story, a conscious relation of character to social background, a moving narrative structurally bound up with character-development. All these elements are present. Between the compass of *The Pilgrim's Progress* and of *The Life and Death of Mr. Badman* the whole bourgeois novel is included.

24

Bedford Corporation

BUNYAN'S basic work was now done; but he still had it in him to produce a fourth prose-experiment which, though not so fertile in its suggestions and implications as the other three great works we have considered, was to give valuable completion to his vision. This was the allegory *The Holy War*. In this he inverted the method of *The Pilgrim's Progress*. In the latter work he had used the theme of the lonely and isolated salvationist to depict the bustling world in which he himself had come to grace. In *The Holy War* he used the image of a whole society to express the psychology of the individual of his day. It is not too much to see in this duality of method in the allegories an intuition of the contradictions in which either approach involved the symbolist. Having used the individual to express society, he wanted to see if he could grapple with the issues more successfully by using society to express the individual.

In *The Holy War* he thus pioneered yet another method. He allegorically anticipated the collective-novel in which the subject is not the individual, but the group.[1] We could have no better example of

[1] Allegories such as Phineas Fletcher's *Purple Island*, which also treat the individual as a cosmic or social organism, lack this creative quality of Bunyan's work; for as we shall see, Bunyan, in seeking to grasp the drama of the individual, defined a dynamic social pattern.

the extraordinary fecundity of the tinker's mind than this capacity of his to throw out in forms at once sketchy and decisive the basic lines of the whole of bourgeois fiction, and to look beyond even that achievement to an art-form in which the social group would be the primary subject-matter.

And all these mighty experiments, so pregnant with æsthetic possibilities, were the work of a man concerned purely with propaganda.

The theme of *The Holy War* is easily told. Mansoul is a city which has been living in innocent happiness; it is invaded and perverted by a band of Diabolonians. It is rescued and restored to its former liberty of love. But the Diabolonians do not give up hope. They make another assault, try to corrupt the city, are defeated, conspire with malcontents, and are yet again defeated.

Thus Bunyan ostensibly seeks to show the fall of the soul and its redemption ; but what he actually does is to give a picture of the social convulsions of his age. However, to understand the roots of his allegory in the history of his times we must consider what had been going on during the last few years.

There had been the nation-shaking matter of the Popish Plot. As a Protestant who recognized in the Papacy the supreme upholder of magic and feudalism, Bunyan would have been much moved by the fear of Catholic domination. The movement into industrialism had not yet irresistibly set in ; and men rightly feared that even now the monarchy might achieve absolutism, as had happened in France. The idea of Plots was therefore in his and every Protestant's mind. In Scotland the attempts to enforce episcopacy had brought about active rebellion ; and Bunyan could not but be in sympathy with the Covenanters. In 1681 the King had dissolved Parliament and begun a vigorous assault on the liberties of his people. Discontent was strong, and the year after Bunyan's *Holy War* appeared there was the Rye-House Conspiracy to murder the King.

The King's efforts to undermine liberty were shrewdly calculated. He set to work to get control of the town-corporations and to use this control to pack any future Parliaments with his adherents. First, therefore, he had to destroy the municipal charters. London was attacked, and soon succumbed. But the happenings at Bedford are what most interest us ; for Bunyan would not only be extremely concerned about them, he later himself became directly involved with the royal scheme. The attack on the Bedford Corporation was not finished during the period when Bunyan was writing his book, but it had begun ; and we can detect throughout his narrative his absorption in the events of the day.

Charles had dissolved Parliament in March 1681, and a few weeks later an Order in Council was issued dealing with inquiries about the Bedford Corporation. The two chamberlains were found to have not taken sacrament at church within twelve months of their election. They were suspended unless they should qualify. Later in the year Robert Audley, the Deputy-Recorder, was accused before the Council at Whitehall of being a supporter of the dissenting conventicles and leader of the disaffected. The Earl of Ailesbury, Lord Lieutenant of the county, moved that Audley and other disaffected aldermen should be removed from their position according to the Corporation Act.

Audley appeared at Whitehall and made a sturdy defence of his behaviour. Among other matters he spoke up on behalf of Bunyan and his conventicle ; and was able to defeat the motion of the Earl of Ailesbury. However, he was deprived of the right to vote in any of the Corporation's assemblies ; and soon we find him displaced.

In October 1583 the full assault was launched by the King. He packed fifty-three of his adherents into the Corporation, and next month another twenty-three. He could now do as he wished with the Corporation. The servile aldermen voted for the surrender of their charter. A new charter was granted, in which the Crown took absolute control of the municipality and in return gave the right to hold two fairs a year !

The Holy War is full of references to the Corporation of Mansoul and to the aldermen of the town :

You have also to the terror of the town of Mansoul threatened with great and sore destruction to punish this Corporation, if she consents not to do as your wills would have her. . . .

The Diabolonians cried up old Incredulity, Forget-good, the new aldermen, and their great one Diabolus. . . .

(*Mr. Incredulity, a Diabolonian speaking*) My lord, quoth he, a couple of peevish gentlemen, that have, as a fruit of their bad dispositions, and, as I fear, through the advice of one Mr. Discontent, tumultuously gathered this company against me this day ; and also attempted to run the town into acts of rebellion against our prince. . . .

There remained in several lurking places of the Corporation many of the old Diabolonians, that either came with the tyrant when he invaded and took the town, or had there by reason of unlawful mixtures their birth and breeding and bringing up.

If one reads these passages in the light of the King's attack on the municipal liberties one can have no doubt where Bunyan's sympathies lay. The Diabolonians are the King's party.

That this assumption is correct is proved beyond argument by the part which the Recorder plays in the allegory. He is an important character among the people of Mansoul, and when Diabolus starts to re-model the town of Mansoul, setting up one man and putting down another at his pleasure, he throws the Recorder, whose name is Conscience, out of his position.

For as for Mr. Recorder, he was a man of courage and faithfulness to speak truth at every occasion, and he had a tongue as bravely hung as he had a head filled with judgement. Now this man Diabolus could by no means abide, because he could not by all wiles, trials, stratagems, and devices that he could use make him wholly his own.

Who can doubt that this Recorder is Deputy-Recorder Robert Audley who stood up and spoke out the truth at the very Council in Whitehall, putting in a word of strong goodwill for Bunyan himself? Diabolus is seen to be Charles II.

The bedrock of *The Holy War* is, then, an imaginative rendering of the conflict between the King and the town of Bedford, absolutism against the liberties of the people.

25

Mansoul

MANSOUL is the Corporation of Bedford ; it is also the society of the godly united against the feudalist foe. Therefore, in telling of the struggle, Bunyan draws on both the immediate facts of the Bedford resistance to absolutist aggression and his memories of the Civil War.

First let us deal with the immediate struggle. We know that the Popish Plot was a bogus-scare ; but the emotions it aroused were based in reality, as appeared when James II came to the throne. The Catholic Church represented feudal reaction ; and its triumph in England would have annihilated all the gains of the long revolutionary struggle of the people. Bunyan and his fellow-dissenters must have had many an anxious discussion on the news of plots and baffled coups that filled the air. His picture of the Diabolonians plotting to overthrow the successful godly of Mansoul is drawn directly from contemporary rumours.

Then stood forth Mr. Diligence and said, ' My lord, as I was upon my watch such a night at the head of Bad Street in this town, I chanced to hear a muttering within this gentleman's house ; then thought I, what's to do here ? So I went up close, but very softly to the side of the house to listen, thinking, as indeed it fell out, that I might light upon some Diabolonian conventicle. So, as I said, I drew nearer and nearer, and when I was got up close to the wall, it was but a while before I perceived that there were outlandish men in the house (but I did well understand their speech, for I have been a traveller myself); now hearing such language in such a tottering cottage as this old gentleman dwelt in, I clapt mine ear to a hole in the window and there heard them talk as follows. . . .'

But throughout the book are scattered details drawn from the Civil War. The accounts of the battles are confused versions of Old Testament warfare and contemporary methods ; but every now and then the civil-war soldier stands out. We have already quoted the description of the soldiers drilling ; and the book is littered with terms drawn directly from civil-war memories. There are sequestration of the estates of the Diabolonians; there are rendezvous —a term much in use during the Civil War, evoking memories of the struggle of the Agitators against the Council of War ; there is a lively account of Diabolonian atrocities which reads like an account by a Roundhead of the behaviour of Prince Rupert's troops (mixed with stories of the Irish Rebellion) ; and the demolishing of fortifications after the Diabolonian outbreak is suppressed refers to the breaking down of fortifications (which Bunyan had seen at the end of the Civil War); there are references to Reformadoes and to Beacons and to army words of command, ' They neither sound boot and saddle, nor horse and away, nor a charge '. The Beacons would be those running along the hilltops of the Chilterns, which were used to signal any enemy advance.

But what is more interesting to us than the mere recrudescence of civil-war memories is the uprush of revolutionary emotion that accompanies them. The pattern of the book becomes plain. It is the pattern of history as Bunyan had known it. As one of the godly he conceives the Civil War as an attack made by the King on the people—as indeed it was. This Diabolonian attack is frustrated ; and for a while all is well ; the Commonwealth rules. Then the Diabolonians make another attack, using more insidious forms ; and this is the attack of Charles II, representing feudal reaction, on the revolutionary gains of the middle and lower classes. It is unthinkable for Bunyan that such an attack should succeed, and so the book ends with the fresh triumph of the people of Mansoul. He thus prophesies the revolution of 1688, which he did not live to see. And also, in the dim future, the day of full social unity.

There are certain confusions in the concepts of the book, resulting from the class-position of Bunyan. As reconciled, he had accepted the insurmountable contradictions of his day ; and part of those contradictions was the fact that there had to be a State. Emotionally he repudiated the State, the ' Law ', accepting as a final arbiter only the rule of grace or love, the dynamic sense of unity evolving from the productive advance. Therefore, while developing the ideology of the petty-bourgeois in their active rôle as creators of industrialism, he yet feels himself essentially a rebel. His deepest impulse is expressed in the letter to a persecuted member of the church : ' Brother, be always looking into the perfect Law of liberty and continue therein. The customs of the people are vain.' Throughout *The Pilgrim's Progress* runs a passionate denunciation of those who live by the Law of good works—that is, the morality of the world, instead of the perfect law of liberty.

Hence his picture of Mansoul as a static community on whom the Diabolonians make repeated assaults is opposed to his deeper sense of revolutionary activity that fights for the perfect law of liberty. And this contradiction comes to a head when he makes the Diabolonians introduce, as one of their last wiles, a corrupting abundance in the town of Mansoul. He fails to distinguish the destiny of his class as increasers of productive power, from the squandering parasitism of the class that battens on the increase. This contradiction is everywhere implicit in the doctrine of Thrift which we have discussed. For by that doctrine the poorer classes accept a discipline that enables them to advance the human whole, but the gainers from this advance are precisely those who have done least to bring it about.

But though Bunyan brings in the movement towards abundance from the wrong angle in his story, yet we must note the approach towards a dialectical understanding of history which he shows by introducing this problem as something that has resulted from the clash of the townfolk and the Diabolonians, the productive lower classes and the feudalists.[1]

---

[1] The core of the ideological confusion is to be found in the fact that the people of Mansoul while fighting for liberty are also fighting for 'King Shaddai', the patriarchal symbol which is in fact common to both Protestant-progressive and Catholic-feudalist, even though each side makes a different use of it.

But the most interesting element that appears in this up-surge of revolutionary emotion in Bunyan is the profound wish, everywhere evident, for revolutionary action. We realize that he has accepted the doctrine of reconciliation only because of his intuition of the overwhelming forces massed, at that period of time, against any attempt to actualize human unity. Underneath, he longs for the active revolutionary struggle. He depicts with the heartiest of joyful accord the ruthless suppression of the Diabolonians.

For instance, Captain Self-denial, finding the towns-folk seduced into partiality towards Mr. Self-love, ' took him from the crowd, and had him among the soldiers, and there he was brained '. This was a ' brave act '. The righteous folk of Mansoul are everywhere conceived as Puritan revolutionaries.

Bunyan feels that his own entire lack of self-pity over the twelve and a half years' jailing he suffered gives him the right to retort on the oppressors their own methods :

These two (Covetousness and Lasciviousness), the captains and elders of the town of Mansoul took, and committed them to custody under the hand of Mr. Trueman the jailer ; and this man handled them so severely, and loaded them so well with irons, that in time they both fell into a very deep consumption and died in the prison-house ; their masters also, according to the agreement of the captains and elders, were brought to take penance in the open place to their shame . . .

Lord Willbewill . . . took Fooling in the street and hanged him up in Wantwit-alley, over against his own house. This Fooling was he that would have had the town of Mansoul deliver up Captain Credence into the hands of Diabolus. . . .

He takes the two young Diabolonians, for such they were (for their father was a Diabolonian born), and has them to Eye-gate, where he raised a very high cross just in the face of Diabolus and of his army, and there he hanged the young villains in defiance to Captain Past-hope, and of the horrible standard of the tyrant. Now this Christian act of the brave Lord Willbewill did greatly abash Captain Past-hope, discourage the army of Diabolus, put fear into the Diabolonian runagates in Mansoul. . . .

And there is no part of the book written with such keen and vivid enjoyment as the description of the trials of the Diabolonians, ending, ' So they crucified the Diabolonians that had been a plague, a grief, and an offence to the town of Mansoul '.

One cannot doubt after reading these passages that the Puritan revolutionary remained intact in Bunyan, suppressed only because of the intuition that the day of wrath and judgment was not yet come. In a passage such as the following we can hear his joy in the cheers that had greeted, near forty years previously, the news that Charles I had surrendered to the Scots :

You cannot think, unless you had been there (as I was,) what a shout there was in Emmanuel's camp when they saw the tyrant bound by the hand of their noble prince, and tied to his chariot wheels.

He expresses his class-position as a labourer when he makes the man chosen as an ambassador to the prince (Christ, human unity) a poor man, Mr. Desires-awake.

MANSOUL

' He dwelt in a very mean cottage in Mansoul, and he came at his neighbours' request.'

Undoubtedly the reason why Bunyan was so much drawn into expressing so nakedly his revolutionary self in this book was the form of fiction he had adopted. Since Mansoul is allegorically the individual imagined as a social organism, the suppression and crucifixion of the reactionaries are presented as meaning only that the individual curbs his baser impulses—that is, achieves class-discipline on the lines we have already analysed. But in fact the book is a definition of the stages of the Protestant revolution; and the fiction of Mansoul as the Body of a single man is preserved only in the names of the gates, Eye, Mouth, Nose, and Ear, and a few such details.

Indeed, so intent is Bunyan on following out the lines of history that he forgets a basic principle of his Calvinism : that he who is truly redeemed by grace cannot fall again. If he were only following out the dogmatic thesis, then how could the soul continue to be so dreadfully threatened, after having been once decisively redeemed from Diabolus? Yet in the story the triumphant redemption solves nothing. At once Carnal-security starts undermining the town's resistances ; the corruption of riches is tried ; and then the army of Bloodmen, the accumulated forces of reaction, pour in on the weakened town. All this is very relevant to the historical scene ; it has many touches of keen analytic insight into social and personal trials and tensions ; but it does not fit in with the Calvinist dogma of predestinated grace. So intent is Bunyan in following out the historical pattern that he introduces the Great Plague as one of the events during the Diabolonian triumph.

The allegory shows the same dilemma here as in *The Pilgrim's Progress*. In both cases the whole complex world of social activity is mirrored in the individual as if it were all only a reflection of his faculties and emotions. Whereas in fact all those faculties and emotions would have no meaning at all without the social world in which the individual has grown to consciousness of himself.

In this dilemma Bunyan was expressing the same difficulty as was shortly to face the bourgeois philosophers who sought to define reality. Locke, by reducing everything to complexes of sense-relations, opened the way to the varying scepticisms of Berkeley and Hume. If one knows, not objects, but only sense-relations, then one knows only one's own reactions and has no means of proving the truth of one's ideas about the world.

Bunyan thus comprehensively covers the whole of the contradictions of bourgeois thought. On the one side is the concrete application to an historical task ; on the other is the individualism, which, by losing touch with the social whole, undermines and queries the objectivity that the first element is building up. From the realistic and socially-active side came Defoe ; from the side that was forced back into a private world came Sterne. And between Defoe and Sterne we have the whole gamut of creative writing during the capitalist epoch. In Bunyan the two aspects are fused.

But this very intensity of his also carries him beyond the whole capitalist epoch. The urgency of his Pilgrim's search for fellowship leads into communism. His sustained effort to define the individual in terms of social organism was expression of the intuited fact that the individual can be fully explained or understood only in terms of the social whole. And that is a realization that leads into Marxism.

The contradiction between the allegory of the individual and the representation of social reality in *The Holy War* comes out into the open at the end of the book. The salvation-by-grace has as its point the rescue from sin altogether. George Fox always held strongly to this attitude, which one might define as an abstraction from the fact that the revolutionary advance is a leap into an entirely new quality. Bunyan, feeling the incongruities of his allegory as a picture of the individual ' soul ', thus made Emmanuel explain his reasons for allowing all the swarm of sins and malcontent resentments to survive within Mansoul which he has redeemed :

O my Mansoul, should I slay all them within, many there be without that would bring thee into bondage ; for were all those within cut off, those without would find thee sleeping, and then, as in a moment, they would swallow up my Mansoul. I therefore left them in thee, not to do thee hurt (the which they yet will, if thou hearken to them and serve them), but to do thee good, the which they must, if thou watch and fight against them.

This argument—that sins are necessary to the redeemed soul—is theologically lunatic ; but it is full of meaning if we take Mansoul as a social image.

Then we see it as an effort to define the necessity of struggle, the interpenetration of opposites, the fusion and breaking apart and re-fusion of social forces.

Bunyan himself always personally accepted the idea of struggle as involving an inner as well as an outer clash, and as being necessary for development. 'God who had much work for him to do', said one who knew him in his later years of successful preaching, 'was still hewing and hammering him by his Word, and sometimes also by more than ordinary temptations and desertions'. He himself stated that he needed a 'maul', and he felt that the moment struggle ceased, everything became meaningless. His preaching triumphs had no meaning to him unless they were part of a conflict. 'Is it so much to be a fiddle?' he asked.

While dealing with *The Holy War*, one may point out that the uprush of revolutionary emotion was accompanied by a rejection of political action as far as a conscious statement of programme went. For instance, in *Seasonable Counsel*, 1684, and the posthumous *Antichrist and his Ruin*. This mixture of a revolutionary emotional core with an acceptance of historically conditioned process is the whole dynamic basis of the compromise included in Grace. The doctrine of withdrawal from politics rules in 1684 when effective political action is impossible. How different is this attitude from that of the godly of Bedfordshire who in 1657 protested strongly against any reversion to monarchy, stating 'the form of a Commonwealth as opposed to Monarchy to be more expedient, yea,

necessary. . . . We declare that we still remain
faithful to the first good cause '. But that was under
the Commonwealth when, despite the anomalies of
State-form, there was a reality of contact between the
Government and the masses.

It was mentioned earlier that in the concept of
Mansoul Bunyan was taking up a basic concept of
medieval popular pulpit-allegory. The use of the
figure of Mansoul in English preaching can be traced
back to a sermon on the so-called Lambeth homilies
compiled near the end of the twelfth century. A
cognate image was that of the Virgin Mary as a
Castle, which we find in a sermon of St. Anselm
(eleventh century) and which went into general use.
It was based on the text of Luke x. 38, *Intravit Jesus
in Castellum*. This fantastic interpretation of the
text shows the idea of house as body and room and
womb which we discuss elsewhere as universal dream-
symbols.

But though Bunyan was thus resuming the medieval
symbol with its deep roots in folk-culture, he was
giving it an entirely new definition ; he coloured and
shaped it in terms of the historical events of his age.

26

The Realistic Content

IN 1684 Bunyan published a sequel or second part of *The Pilgrim's Progress*. He tells how Christian's wife and children follow in the same track to the City of Light. The story is able to stand worthily at the side of the first part ; if it lacks the creative novelty of the first Progress, it has elements of equable good-humour and sympathy that its more fiery predecessor lacked. Christian has blazed the way ahead, and his family do not meet such terrors, though they would scarcely get through if they were not accompanied by Mr. Greatheart.

We have already dealt with the contradictions that Christiana's adventures show in common with the other allegorical tales ; but we can deal here with the richness of realistic detail that makes all these tales so effective. One and all, they are inhabited by the people whom Bunyan had known ; and we are given a vivid picture of crowded lower-class life of the mid-seventeenth century. The brimming sense of life burst the allegorical forms, and the impression left on us is in no way one of labelled abstractions, but of the busy Bedford life among which the books were written.

THE REALISTIC CONTENT

Especially can we see that the forthright type of Puritan soldier, the revolutionary of the day, had indelibly impressed Bunyan. He is never happier than when depicting someone like Greatheart, Faithful, or Valiant, or Captain Experience.

Then said Greatheart to Mr. Valiant-for-Truth, ' Thou hast worthily behaved thyself; let me see thy sword '. So he showed it to him.

When he had taken it in his hand, and looked thereon a while, he said, ' Ha, it is a right Jerusalem blade '.

Valiant : ' It is so. Let a man have one of these blades, with a hand to wield it, and skill to use it ; and he may venture upon an angel with it. He need not fear its holding, if he can but tell how to lay on. Its edges will never blunt. It will cut flesh and bones, and soul and spirit, and all '.

Greatheart : ' But you fought a great while ; I wonder you was not weary '.

Valiant : ' I fought till my sword did cleave to my hand ; and when they were joined together, as if a sword grew out of my arm, and when the blood ran through my fingers, then I fought with most courage '.

How he kindles when he deals with this type of the Puritan militant :

' But here was great odds, three against one.'

' 'Tis true ; but little and more are nothing to him that has the truth on his side. Though an host should encamp against me, said one, my heart shall not fear : though war should rise against me, in this I will be confident.'

And here is the revolutionary's testament :

' My sword I give to him that shall succeed me in my pilgrimage, and my courage and skill to him that can get it. My marks and scars I carry with me, to be a witness for me, that I have fought his battles, who now shall be my rewarder.'

Thus acts Captain Experience :

Now they left Captain Experience in the town, because he was yet ill of his wounds which the Diabolonians had given him in the last fight. But when he perceived that the captains were at it, what does he but calling for his crutches with haste, gets up, and away he goes to the battle, saying, ' Shall I lie here when my brethren are in the fight, and when Emmanuel the Prince will show himself in the field to his servants ? '

But when the enemy saw the man come with his crutches, they were daunted yet the more ; for, thought they, what spirit has possessed these Mansoulians that they fight me upon their crutches ?

And the noblest passage in all his works is the paragraph telling of the end of Faithful, after the powerfully satirical picture of the trial in Vanity Fair :

They therefore brought him out, to do with him according to their law ; and first, they scourged him, then they buffeted him, then they lanced his flesh with knives ; after that, they stoned him with stones, then pricked him with their swords, and, last of all, they burned him to ashes at the stake. Thus came Faithful to his end.

Not a word more. What is not said is fiercely eloquent with all the stoicism of Bunyan's own sufferings for the Truth.

All the details in this allegorical world are concrete. There is a welcome dish of milk well-crumbed for the tired wanderers, and Greatheart, like any other good soldier, has a map of the campaigning country ; he strikes a light from his tinder-box to have a look at the map in the dark. Madam Bubble is tall and comely, swarthy-skinned, smooth-speaking, with a smile at the end of each sentence ; and she keeps fingering the money inside the purse at her side. When Christiana's small son refuses the pill after getting a belly-ache from eating fruit, she has to touch it with the tip of her tongue to prove it isn't horrid. The men who are mending the King's highway fill up with dung and muck instead of with durable material. And so on. Mr. False-peace sounds a dry enough conception ; but here is the picture of him as a child :

I was his play-fellow, only I was somewhat older than he ; and when his mother did use to call him home from his play, she used to say, ' False-peace, False-peace, come home quick, or I'll fetch you '. Yea, I knew him when he was sucked ; though I was then but little, yet I can remember that when his mother did use to sit at the door with him, or did play with him in her arms, she would call him twenty times, together, ' My little False-peace, my pretty False-peace ', and ' O my sweet rogue, False-peace ', and again, ' O my little bird, False-peace,' and ' How do I love my child ! ' The gossips also know it is thus, though he has had the face to deny it in open Court.

When Mansoul has to be guarded, the citizens set guards at the gates, and prudently double them on market-days. When they are rescued from the first inroad of tyranny, they are feasted by the Son ; and are delighted like rustics at a rich corporation-dinner :

When a fresh dish was set before them, they would whisperingly say to each other, What is it ? for they wist not what to call it. They drank also of the water that was made wine, and were very merry with him.

Mercy is courted by Mr. Brisk ; he sees how active a worker she is, but does not know that all she does is for charity :

'Nay then', said Mercy, 'I will look no more on him ; for I purpose never to have a clog to my soul '.

Prudence then replied, that there needed no great matter of discouragement to be given to him ; her continuing so as she had begun to do for the poor, would quickly cool his courage.

So, the next time he comes, he finds her at her old work, a-making of things for the poor. Then said he, ' What ! always at it ? '

' Yes ', said she, ' either for myself or for others '.

' And what canst thou earn a day ? ' quoth he.

' I do these things ', said she, ' that I may be rich in good works, laying up in store for myself a good foundation against the time to come, that I may lay hold on eternal life '.

' Why, prithee, what does thou with them ? ' said he.

' Clothe the naked ', said she.

With that his countenance fell. So he forbore to come at her again. And when he was asked the reason why, he said, ' That Mercy was a pretty lass, but troubled with ill conditions '.

This passage shows very well, in small compass, the way that Bunyan makes his allegory coincide with the actual life of his class, so that his Puritan revaluation builds directly on the facts of existence as known to the people he addresses. Hence the tremendous success that his work had among that chosen audience.

This was the kind of thing that the lower-middle and lower classes had wanted when they shouted at the hierarchical clergy that they were dumb dogs. (It is an interesting example of the unity of the whole

Protestant movement that as early as 1216 we find one Jacques de Vitry writing of the Franciscans, ' I believe it is to shame the prelates, who are like dogs unable to bark, that God wills, before the end of the world, to save many souls by these poor simple ones '.) In these allegories the people could recognize themselves and their associates in all their strength and weakness, while the unrelenting lesson of class-discipline supported them in their trials and uncertainties.

Bunyan made several attempts to write verse, but without any distinction. However, in two lyrics he did succeed in catching a musical tension of form, a sweetness distilled from the broken heart of reconciliation in a world of evil (class-oppression) plus the forward-driving spirit of his class. Both are from the second part of the *Progress* :

> He that is down, needs fear no fall ;
> He that is low, no pride ;
> He that is humble, ever shall
> Have God to be his guide.
> I am content with what I have,
> Little it be or much ;
> And, Lord, contentment still I crave,
> Because thou savest such.
> Fullness to such a burden is
> That go on pilgrimage ;
> Here little, and hereafter bliss,
> Is best from age to age.

The conscious class-reference of this poem is established by the statement closely preceding it : ' Behold how green this valley is, also how beautiful with lilies. I have also known many labouring men that have got good estates in this Valley of Humiliation.'

The second poem is of further interest in making evident that Bunyan had glanced at Shakespeare's plays, or at least at *As You Like It* :

Who would true valour see,
Let him come hither ;
One here will constant be,
Come wind, come weather.
There's no discouragement
Shall make him once relent
His first avowed intent
To be a pilgrim.

Whoso beset him round
With dismal stories,
Do but themselves confound ;
His strength the more is.
No lion can him fright,
He'll with a giant fight,
But he will have a right
To be a pilgrim.

Hobgoblin nor foul fiend
Can daunt his spirit ;
He knows he at the end
Shall life inherit.
Then fancies, fly away,
He'll fear not what men say,
He'll labour night and day
To be a pilgrim.

The bliss hereafter is that light of perfect comradeship which had shone for Bunyan in his dream beyond the obstructing pressures of history.

27

Death

WITH the accession of James II to the throne in 1685 the royal attack on the nation intensified. Bedford, as a result of Charles II's strategy, was, like so many other municipalities, in the hands of the Crown. In the autumn occurred Monmouth's rebellion, with which we may suppose Bunyan to have been in sympathy. That he felt a growing sense of insecurity is proved by a deed which he executed in December. Wishing to ensure that his wife and family would be safe from poverty if he should be once more persecuted, he drew up this deed conveying all his property to her. He still calls himself Brazier, but, as he mentions ' debts (owing to him), ready money, plate, rings, household stuff, apparel, utensils, brass, pewter, bedding and all other my substance ', we can see that he was considerably better off than in the lean days when he set up house with his first wife. Though he calls himself Brazier, we may be sure that he had not practised his craft for many years ; though his oldest son, also a brazier, was doubtless carrying on the family tradition in a forge.

To strengthen the Crown's hand, James went on with his brother's trick of getting control of the boroughs ; he decided further to eject all J.P.'s or other county officers who were not subservient to the Crown. As the Catholics and outright royalists were too much in a minority to provide a stable basis for the Crown's reactionary policy, James decided to work on his brother's method of splitting the Protestant opposition by offering toleration to the dissenters. At Bedford Lord Ailesbury, King's man, got in touch, through an intermediary, with Bunyan and another leading dissenter. Bunyan, though aware of the reasons for the King's attitude, was ready to take any concessions that could be extorted ; and agreed to support ' only such members of Parliament as will certainly vote for repealing all the Tests and Penal Laws touching Religion '. This meant that the weight of the dissenting leaders would go ' to steer all their friends and followers accordingly '—on the King's side. It is worth noting that Foster, the arch-persecutor of dissenters for twenty-five years, answered a royal questionnaire on the question of toleration : ' He submits all to His Majesty's Pleasure ' ; he was ready to make a complete volte-face to curry favour.

In January 1688, and in March, the King set to work to pack into the Bedford Corporation the dissenters who were ready to back him, at least with regard to religious toleration. Six or seven were members of Bunyan's congregation. There can thus be no doubt that Bunyan was ready to countenance any steps that would lead to religious freedom ; but at the same time his knowledge of the King's duplicity made him refuse to take any active part in supporting the King. He flatly turned down all overtures, and refused even to meet the King's emissary, who was probably the new Earl of Ailesbury.

His fellow-dissenters had only a short stay on the borough Council ; but while they were there they did some good work in attacking abuses. For instance, they outraged several previous mayors by demanding that they should disemburse all the charity-money that they had embezzled.

Bunyan had been living through these years on the east side of Bedford, in a small parish of forty-seven families—in 1673-4 when the Hearth Tax roll was taken. We catch a glimpse of him at home in the diary of the antiquary Hearne :

I heard Mr. Bagford, some time before he died, say that he walked once into the country, on purpose to see the study of John Bunyan. When he came, John received him very civilly and courteously ; but his study consisted only of a Bible and a parcel of books, *The Pilgrim's Progress* chiefly, all lying on a shelf or shelves.[1]

In April 1668 there was a commotion at Bedford. Two fires broke out, one in the night, the other next morning at a malthouse close to Bunyan's house. ' Persons were much singed and burnt by the sheets of flame driven in their faces through the fury of the wind.'

Bunyan had been for some time now well known at London. We find him preaching at Pinner's Hall, a city-company hall often used by Nonconformists, and before the socially-important congregation of his friend Owen in Moorfields. He seems to have been very friendly with a Lord Mayor, for an incorrect

[1] Bagford was a printer and bookseller.

notion grew up that he had been this Mayor's chaplain. A prettily-inlaid cabinet remains of presents that were given him. Various offers were made that would have been financially to his advantage, but he always answered, ' I dwell among my own people '. When he preached in London, if a day's notice was given, he obtained an audience that overflowed the meeting-house. Once he had to enter by a back door and be pulled almost over people before he could get to the pulpit, so crammed was the hall.

There is an interesting account of his preaching by John Doe, who edited his works after his death. From this we get a glimpse of the needs to which Bunyan was ministering. His hearers were not seeking for ' the historical or doing-for-favour '—that is, the mere chronicle-exposition of the Old Testament, or the crude doctrine of success that salved capitalist consciences. They wanted the conviction of ' love and the promises '—that is, the sense that their struggles would bring forth fruits of unity.

It was at this time of persecution (1685–6) that I heard Mr. Bunyan came to London sometimes and preached; and because of his fame, and I having read some of his books, I had a mind to hear him. And accordingly I did at Mr. More's meeting in a private house; and his text was, ' The fears of the wicked shall come upon him, but the desires of the righteous shall be granted'. But I was offended at the text, because not a New Testament one, for then I was very jealous of being cheated by men's sophisticating of Scripture to serve their turn or opinion, I being then come into New Testament light in the love of God and the promises, having had enough of the historical and doing for favour in the Old Testament.

DEATH

But Mr. Bunyan went on, and preached so New Testament like that he made me admire, and weep for joy, and give him my affections. And he was the first man that ever I heard preach to my unenlightened understanding and experience, for methought all his sermons were adapted to my condition, and had apt similitudes, being full of the love of God and the manner of its secret working upon the soul, and of the soul under the sense of it, that I could weep for joy most part of his sermons ; and so, by a letter, I introduced myself into his acquaintance, and, indeed, I have not since met with a man that I liked so well.

In August 1688 Bunyan set out on his last journey from Bedford to London. He was not riding direct, but meant to make a circuit to Reading, where he had, according to tradition, preached in the time of persecution, disguised as a carter.

This time he had not come merely to preach : he had promised a young man to intercede with his father for him. This young man had angered his father, who had sworn to disinherit him. Bunyan pacified the old man, and then set off for London. He wanted to see through the press the proofs of his latest doctrinal work, *The Acceptable Sacrifice*. Heavy rain came on ; and by the time he had finished the 40 miles ride he was soaked to the skin. He had arranged to stay with a friend, John Strudwick, grocer, who lived in a plain four-storeyed house on Snow Hill near Newgate, with a Star as business-sign.

He preached on Sunday in Whitechapel, but on Tuesday fell into a fever of some kind, and lay abed sick for ten days. Then he died, serenely, on the last day of August. He was buried in Bunhill Fields, the great London burial-ground of dissenters.

He left goods to the value of £49 19s.; and on this sum and what came in from his books his widow lived for the year and a half before she too died. Of his six children, the blind Mary had already died. Elizabeth, John, and Thomas survived, children of his first marriage ; and Sarah and Joseph, of his second marriage. John joined his father's church in 1693, later becoming a moderately active member. The fact that he had not joined during his father's lifetime suggests that there had been some discord between them.

A dissenter who had known Bunyan thus described his appearance :

He was tall of stature, strong-boned, though not corpulent, somewhat of a ruddy face, with sparkling eyes, wearing his hair on his upper lip after the old British fashion ; his hair reddish, but in his later days time had sprinkled it with grey ; his nose well set, but not declining or bending, and his mouth moderately large ; his forehead something high, and his habit always plain and modest.

He adds that though he looked ' of a stern and rough temper ' he was in conversation ' mild and affable, not given to loquacity or much discourse in company, unless some urgent occasion required it '. And another friend speaks of his face striking ' something of awe into them that had nothing of the fear of God '.

The sketch of his face by Robert White agrees with the verbal picture, except that there is not much suggestion of the awe-striking aspect. Rather do we see the vigorous, almost-jovial man who had so shrewd an eye for the facts of life about him ; though we can well imagine the vivid eyes in anger full of cold fire and command.

28

Endpiece

WHEN Philip Henslowe, pawnbroker and brothel-landlord, decided in 1592 to keep accounts of the Rose Theatre, which he owned, he wrote at the top of the page, 'Jesus 1592'; and when a couple of pages later he started a new account, he began with the entry, 'In the name of God'. There, in caricature-simplified form, we have one side of Protestantism. This side was amply served by the leading Protestant preachers. But there was another side, as has been demonstrated by the tale of Bunyan in this book. That other side was the insurgent sense of unity.

We have seen how in 1649 there occurred the first grand division in the Protestant movement in England. The bourgeois, having won to power, renounced everything in Protestantism that savoured of insurgency. Throughout the next two centuries that process of division went on repeating itself, though in less dramatic fashion. The bourgeoisie went over to what Bunyan calls with contempt the 'national Church'. That Church became instantly moribund. For instance, late in the eighteenth century, when Miss Hannah More started investigating the literacy of country parishes, she reported,

JO BUNYAN, WHOSE FAMILY ON BOTH SIDES HAVE BEEN
OVER A HUNDRED YEARS IN THE 'WOOD'

He is now waging a Holy War for Portland Town

ENDPIECE

'We saw but one Bible in the parish of Cheddar, and that was used to prop a flower-pot'. In 1799 the Rev. Sydney Smith wrote, 'In England (except among ladies in the middle rank of life) there is no religion at all. The clergy of England have no more influence on the people at large than the cheesemongers of England.'

The insurgency had passed entirely over to the Nonconformists; and the process of internal division, as we have mentioned, kept on repeating itself within their ranks. For the class-impulses involved were dual. There was on the one side the section whom the doctrine of thrift was indeed leading to power and purpose; and there was the section who were merely being more uprooted and suppressed, massing into a proletariat.

For the first section the Nonconformist doctrine provided the success-election of the chosen, and resistance to the world of the reprobates. Quakers became big bankers; a majority of the eighteenth-century ironmongers had Puritan connections; the leading Lancashire clothiers were usually Nonconformists. A long line of scientists and inventors, culminating in Faraday, were also Nonconformists. Faraday, for instance, was a Sandemanian, member of a tiny sect intensely strict in their creed that Faith was a gift of God and that Christianity could never become an established religion without being entirely perverted.

Here, then, in Faraday we find an essential doctrinal identity with Bunyan. For the same reasons that creed of Grace and the Law of Liberty recommended itself to working-man and scientist. It gave the basis for reconciliation with an environment against which the individual felt a revolutionary impulse impossible of actualization. The reconciliation was needed so that the individual would have the foothold from which to act and think ; the conviction of grace, of hostility to the accepted ' Law ', preserved the core of revolutionary emotion, abstracting it on to a plane where its contradiction with the reconciliation-basis did not obtrude sufficiently to paralyse the mind.

We see more than ever, then, the purpose served by that fierce rejection of the Law and all its works that burns through every book of Bunyan's, and strongest of all, perhaps, in *The Pilgrim's Progress*.

Thou wast almost choked therewith; this is to show thee that the law, instead of cleansing the heart (by its working) from sin, doth revive, put strength into, and increase it in the soul, even as it doth discover and forbid it, for it doth not give power to subdue.

This is the dilemma of justice in a class-society, where rules of equity are elaborately devised and painstakingly applied to conditions based at every point on oppression. As the dissenter Defoe wrote :

Knowledge of things would teach them every hour
That Law is but a heathen word for Power.

The Law which Bunyan rejects is, of course, more than the mere constituted law of the State : it is rather the whole basis of oppression from which the various laws derive. Hence the complaint that the Law can only multiply sins, can only point them out impotently, but can never cleanse the breeding-heart of sin. Only grace, the sense of human unity, can hope to transcend the antinomies of the State and create a morality which is not tyrannous.

Nobody could seem less a revolutionary than the quiet, laborious, self-immolating Faraday ; yet we see by his close adherence to the Sandemanian sect that he needed the release of belonging to a body of fellowship which absolutely denied the State any right to intrude.

Before we leave this question of the Law, it is of importance to note that under the Commonwealth the recognition of the tyranny of the State-law was widespread. We need not go to the Levellers or Diggers for evidence of this. Cromwell declared : ' The sons of Zeruiah are yet too strong for us. . . . The law, as it is now constituted, serves only to maintain the lawyers, and to encourage the rich to oppress the poor.' There were theorists, such as Chidley or Pryor, who had many intelligent reforms to advocate ; and the ' Parliament of the Saints ', 1653, made strenuous efforts to grapple with the problem of reformation and codification. Here, as in so many ways, the Commonwealth attempted to work reforms which never have been, and never will be achieved under capitalism, since they cut at the whole root by which capitalism supports itself.

So, there were two sides to the Protestant movement—two sides which persisted through all the various changes that overcame dissent across the years. In one sense, for instance, Wesley canalized the revolutionary impulses of the masses in the eighteenth century and sent them to drain away in the arid sands of the religious abstraction. ' The oracles of God ', he said, ' command us to be subject to the higher powers, and that Honour the King is thus connected with the fear of God '. Yet the mass-movements that Wesley compacted were a necessary prelude to the proletarian movements of the next century, and Wesley himself was in the line of Luther and Bunyan as a denouncer of profiteers, cornerers, and forestallers. No revolutionary action was possible in England in the eighteenth century. England was not France, where the bourgeois revolution had yet to come. The dispossessed masses, not yet welded by industrial discipline, needed the religious banner to draw them together, to fuse them with a sense of unity, which, though it held them passive for the time being, yet did at the same time hold the revolutionary core intact though abstracted.

Hence the way we find, during the struggles that led up to Chartism, that official Nonconformity tried to damp down the class-war, but the masses who moved into the forefront of battle were in large part Nonconformists. The Wesleyan preachers of the Bath district in 1839 resolved that any Methodist who joined the Chartists should be thrown out of the Church. The five Dorset labourers who are known to history as the Tolpuddle Martyrs were all rank-and-file Methodists. These contrasting examples serve better than any generalized comment to show how the dissenting impulse worked in two ways. With Chartism we enter on the road leading to full-grown industrial struggle and socialist science ;

and therefore from that point the part played by religious dissent wanes in importance.

The importance of Bunyan's work as a force keeping alive the revolutionary content in dissent cannot be exaggerated. No author was so widely read among the lower-classes of the eighteenth century. His audience was almost entirely working-class. Addison (or someone so like him as to be indistinguishable) said that no matter how bad an author was he found some readers, as witness Quarles and Bunyan. Burke speaks of ' degrading ' a work ' to the style of *The Pilgrim's Progress* '. This is not to say that a sprinkling of more intelligent persons in the upper classes did not read him and appreciate his quality. Dr. Johnson, for one, rated him very high. Swift said, ' I have been better entertained and more informed by a few pages in *The Pilgrim's Progress* than by a long discussion upon the will and the intellect, and simple or complex ideas '.

Still, his audience was the working-class. He was contemned among the refined classes. Cowper felt that it was bad taste even to name Bunyan in print :

> I name thee not, lest so despised a name
> Should move a sneer at thy deserved fame.

It was the working class who took him to their heart ; they needed him. He gave them conviction of worth and ultimate purpose ; he confirmed in them the revolutionary sense that only the perfect Law of Liberty could satisfy.

I have no doubt that William Blake read at least *The Pilgrim's Progress* and learnt there the idiom that his own revolt took : the idiom of wrath against the oppressive Law and the belief that only a morality of love and unity could save. Learnt also to think symbolically in types and forms. I have no doubt that Blake, who belonged to the class that had taken Bunyan to their hearts, read *The Pilgrim's Progress* as a child and was indelibly influenced by it.

But we are not concerned here to trace out Bunyan's influence in detail ; enough to show the main lines on which he continued to affect the masses. We have already seen what tremendous work he did as a literary innovator. He founded the great bourgeois novel ; he first created a prose for narrative purposes which was at once objective in content and highly sensitive in form. He projected in concrete symbols a vision of the revolutionary era through which he had lived, and its glorious significances. He gave us an autobiography which had no parallel except the *Confessions* of Augustine, and which far surpassed Augustine's book in the way it fused, yet held separate, all the complex stages of a protracted inner conflict—though it lacked Augustine's intellectual scope.

Cromwell and Lilburne on the side of political action, Milton and Bunyan on the side of literary expression, were the four great figures embodying at highest tension the drama and meaning of the seventeenth-century revolution. Bunyan gave voice to all the popular feelings of derelict despair, the general stupefaction and suspension, that followed the failure of Lilburne, even among those who had not consciously identified themselves with the Lilburnean cause. He, more than any other man, transmuted that cloudy frustration into an ideological weapon of hope which served the masses well in the difficult century and a half awaiting them.

Coming into the tradition of ' English Letters ', as he did, after a lengthy period when he was considered a mere mechanic writing for mechanics, he has never been given justice. He may have received much academical praise after he was at last conducted into textbooks.[1] (His reception came at the moment when the class-struggle had sharpened to the point where *any* writer with religious professions became respectable ; for the proletarian forces were steadily moving away from the religious formulation, being able to let their sense of unity flow into trade-unions and political agitation. Then was the ripe moment for discovering that the Bedford tinker was a genius.) But, though formally accepted, Bunyan has never been understood. The tinker has never fitted properly into the academic niches.

To understand Bunyan is to understand the English Nonconformist movement. Indeed, one may say that without understanding Bunyan one cannot get to the heart of that movement. Wesley was a greater figure as an evangelist organizer ; and there were several others who could rival Bunyan as a preacher. George Fox, with his wild vein of pantheist poetry and his burning heartache of unity, is

---

[1] The final act of bourgeois falsification was made by Froude. Southey and Macaulay began the process—especially Macaulay ; for Southey, for all his ' renegadism ', remained in essential revolt against capitalism all his life, and was able, at least partially, to intuit the central Bunyan.

a great dissenter. But none is quite so significant as Bunyan. Coming at the moment when the great split occurred in English Protestantism, the abortive Leveller revolt, he was the man who with his powerful imaginative conceptions gave Nonconformity a stable basis of idiom for the next two centuries.

All that was most vital in the English masses was linked up with the dissenting struggle. Bunyan entered deep into the consciousness of the masses. They were all his Pilgrims accepting the toil and the trial because of the warm light of fellowship on the mountains of the future. They were building a house of fellowship, and Bunyan abode with them as a voice of guidance and exhortation. His word was with them as the password of the faithful in a world of environing malignants. The glow in their hearts and the courage of their resistance they felt were owed to him more than to any other one man.

Without understanding Nonconformity one cannot understand the English. The energy that led England out of feudalism while the rest of Europe succumbed in some form or other and only partially stabilized the gains of the Renascence and Reformation; the energy that made England the world's industrial centre for so many generations. All this we owe primarily to the Nonconformists. We cannot blame them for the cruelties and oppressions that accompanied industrialism. In seeking to moralize the process, they did indeed end by sanctifying it ; but we utterly distort the inner meaning of Nonconformity if we see only the sanctifying side. Deepest of all, driving on into the future, was the glow and fire of grace ; and the hope of an effective bond of human unity always burned in the concept of grace, even if sometimes fitfully. That light of grace shone into distant places, into dreams that no class-society could finally satisfy. To understand the English masses even to-day, to realize the warm heart of English Radicalism—in so many ways linked up with dissent [1]—one must go back to Bunyan. Only by grasping the inner meaning of dissent can we realize the traditions of struggle and acceptance so deeply rooted in the English masses. Unless we grasp the historical residuum of dissent, we cannot enter into the English masses of to-day. Now, when the hills of fellowship, the Chilterns delectably floating in a mist of summer light, can at last be reached, we can profitably return to Bunyan ; by carrying his vision to its last steps of implication, we reach the stage where the Birthright once more comes down to earth. Another Lilburne must arise, another Winstanley ; and this time the earthly goal will not be lost, will not be doomed to recede into the summer distance, the horizon of bounteous light.

Thus begins the dream of the Pilgrim. A poor man

[1] It is to the honour of nonconformity that when Bradlaugh was persecuted in every way by the State and the State-Church for his anti-religious propaganda, several nonconformists gave him valuable support in defence of freedom of opinion. But the final bankruptcy of official dissent is to be found in the utter collapse of the ' nonconformist conscience ' on the question of the Fascist attack on Spanish Democracy. One does not deny, however, that the idiom of religious dissent can yet serve as a worthy social stimulus to individuals or groups (*e.g.* the writers of *Towards the Christian Revolution*, 1937, all members of the United Church of Canada, who fully face up to the meaning of social injustice in the world of to-day).

stands facing the world that has dispossessed him, and asking a question.

As I walked through the wilderness of this world, I lighted on a certain place where was a den ; and I laid me down in that place to sleep ; and as I slept I dreamed a dream. I dreamed and behold, I saw a man clothed with rags, standing in a certain place, with his face from his own house, a book in his hand, and a great burden upon his back. I looked and saw him open the book and read therein ; and as he read he wept and trembled, and not being able to contain, he brake out with a lamentable cry, saying, ' What shall I do ? '

Whoever dreams that dream, and faces out its meaning, must come to conclusions that endanger all things but the impulse towards the perfect law of liberty. And that is a sufficient reason why Bunyan should not be understood by the wise men whom he scorned, as he has been understood, emotionally, by countless numbers of the poor and the oppressed.

NOTES

HERE are collected some analyses which, though relevant to the full understanding of the book's thesis, would upset the balance of parts if placed in the body of the book. I therefore place them at the end, as illustrative notes.

1. THE STRUGGLE AGAINST ENCLOSURES

It must not be thought that the peasants tamely submitted to the theft of their land; and as so much of Bunyan's emotion about the lost Birthright related to the loss of the land by the yeomanry, it is important that the mood of the peasants should be understood. Up to the age of sixteen Bunyan lived in a village, and he could not but have heard the question of enclosure discussed with anger and threats of insurrection.

There were two great outbursts of the peasants: that of Jack Ket (discussed in the text) and that of the Midland peasants in 1607, when one Reynolds, nicknamed Captain Pouch, was the leader. The peasants of the Midland counties gathered in large wandering bands, and tore down the fences and hedges, or filled up the dykes and ditches, till they were dispersed by force and their leaders hanged.

But insurrections went on all the while in scattered fashion. There were so many riots in the years immediately preceding the Civil War that one might argue the possessing classes needed the war to crush the peasants as much as the King. In the estates of the Prince of Wales in Cornwall the peasants rioted and pulled down the fences. In Huntingdon the lands of the Queen and the Earl of March were attacked by tenants to the sound of the drum; fences were cast down and ditches filled. (One may pause to note how enclosure had been going on on the royal lands; the King had also enclosed in the Forest of Dean. So we see that the anti-enclosure policy of Laud was only one facet of the royal policy, which as much as the bourgeois methods worked out against the small man in its general bearings.)

There were riots at Hounslow Heath; at West Durham and Wroxham (again lands of the Prince of Wales). The high sheriff of

253

Norfolk tried to overawe the peasants, but they were ' so far from
obeying his commands that they further threatened to destroy all
other improved grounds'. In the spring of 1641 the tumults and
' unlawful assemblies ' in Huntingdonshire were so bad that orders
to disperse were ' not only disobeyed, but contemned and widely
despised '. The Lords had to order trained bands to the scene. The
Earl of Hereford had 160 acres of enclosed land attacked by rioters in
Somerset. In 1640 there had been attacks at Doncaster on the
property of T. Cropley; next year there were five indictments for
similar offences. The cheats and thefts of land produced by the
fen-draining projects caused much disorder and rioting, which
culminated in the large-scale rioting at Epworth. Sir Antony
Thomas's lands in Lincolnshire were attacked, the sluices and sewers
damaged, and ditches filled in.

In July 1641 the Lords noted that daily complaints were received
of violent attacks on enclosures, ' which have been observed to have
been more frequently done since Parliament began than formerly'.
In 1642 we hear of a band of 340 peasants gathering in Durham to
break down enclosures. In April 1643 the lands of the Earl of Suffolk
in Essex were attacked by peasants ' alleging that if they took not
advantage of the Time, they shall never have the opportunity again '.

The Essex peasants were right. The decisive moment of class-
conflict had arrived.

In 1643 there were riots in Somerset, Dorset, Wiltshire. In May
we hear of the peasants of Shenley, Herts, attacking the enclosures
of Captain Edward Wingate, sawing up the gates, digging down the
banks, and setting to work ' to lay all the said land common '. The
Commons authorized the deputy-lieutenants of the county, J.P.s,
constables, or other officers, ' to use their utmost endeavours to
apprehend such disorderly rude persons. . . .'

These details will suffice to show how widespread was the peasant
movement, how deep the resentment, against enclosures.

One set of ideas that accompanied this outburst and found expression among the Lilburneans is of interest. It shows an immature
effort to grasp the class-war. The oppression of the law it attributed
to ' Norman Tyranny'. The ruling class were Normans who had
enslaved the free-born English, and stolen their lands. There was
a modicum of truth in this notion; but it over-simplified things,
imagining pre-Norman England as a perfect clan-brotherhood.

2. UTOPIAS

The imagining of Utopias was part of the revolutionary ferment of
ideas, which made the Commonwealth so greatly anticipate the whole
map of the future. The most interesting writers were Winstanley,
Peter Cornelius, W. Covel, Samuel Hartlib. All these thinkers

devised communist states. Winstanley came closest to a scientific Communism; for he did not conceive his perfect society as static. ' The Law of Freedom ' which he sought to formulate lay in the utilization of science in every relation of human life. He had a profound vision of human unity, and he went to the crux of the matter. His Communists ' see their Freedom lies in plenty and their bondage in poverty '. A disciple of his, John Bellers, directly influenced Owen and thus linked up these imaginations with the Chartist struggles.

One may claim for Winstanley that he is the first scientific Communist, even though his ground-plan is necessarily vague. He never loses sight of the fact that scientific knowledge and the development of technics constitute the basis of freedom, and this awareness is part of a passionate sense of the human bond. He sees the relation between a leisured intellectual class and the needs of the parasites to ' advance themselves to be lords and masters over their labouring brethren . . . which occasions all the trouble in the world '. He has perfect faith in the great flow of human creativeness that will come through the release from fear, once the class-state is ended.

Cornelius gives us a quieter version of Winstanley's intense vision. He thinks of his people as living in collective groups, twenty or thirty families together, with both a town and a country house. The surplus is divided every six or twelve months among all the members; the government is chosen yearly. Like Winstanley, he realizes the need to base his society on a continual advance in technics : ' the only way to find the height, depth, length, and breadth of all things '. He too sees the stimulus that will result when men no longer ' continually hover between hope and fear ' ; and he stands for perfect tolerance of opinion. ' No reason when they do not hinder the common welfare to exclude them from the society.'

Covel also has the idea of collective groups eating together. He wants all charters of incorporation to be revoked and all workers employed upon a common stock. Money he denounces as the thing of evil, which with its machinery of gain and loss hinders you ' from hearing the Voice '. Though vaguer than Winstanley or Cornelius, he sees the human core in the powers of productive union. ' We want method exceedingly in association together in good things, we see it practised in wicked things.'

Hartlib's communist state, which he calls Macaria, is a fantasy based on an awareness of the constructive side of the unloosed capitalist forces. His sketch of a planned economy is a rough prophecy of the Five-Year Plan of the Soviet Union. His idea is that Macaria achieves such perfect efficiency and justice that the rest of the world is drawn in to follow suit. For ' the common people, knowing their own rights and liberties, will not be governed by ways of oppression '.

All these writers, it will be seen, develop the creative aspects

JOHN BUNYAN

of revolutionary capitalism so that they think *through* capitalism into what lies on the other side. They see that once the problem of plenty is solved, the problem of human unity is equally involved.

It is necessary to know about these Utopias when we consider the full ideological content of the Birthright which Bunyan felt he had lost. Though he doubtless knew nothing of the above writers or their ideas—except perhaps whatever garbled account he would have heard of Winstanley and his Diggers—yet the fact that the unity-sense of his day could integrate to such a fine concept as these Utopias show, is of importance in estimating the social tensions reflected in *Grace Abounding*.

3. TRAUMA AND RELEASE (page 178)

This fusion of qualities is the first organic experience of the ' identity of opposites '. In the way that birth becomes symbol and prototype of either obstruction and death or release and successful adjustment, so the notion of identity-of-opposites has two forms.

One is abstract form, based on frustration and fear, in which life is considered irrationally composed of opposites that cancel out one another, that are locked in an irreconcilable struggle never issuing in meaning. Meaning is conceived as a transcendental factor imposed from without on the duality of sense and mind.

In this idiom of the birth-trauma (birth as a wounding experience) the sense of division is so deep that the identity-of-opposites is recognized by it only as a mad paradox deepening the futility of life. The following lines from Kyd's *Spanish Tragedy* excellently sum up this attitude of paradox, for they give the whole scheme of relations involved :

> O eyes ! no eyes, but fountains fraught with tears ;
> O life, no life, but lively form of death ;
> O world, no world, but mass of public wrongs,
> Confused and filled with murders and misdeeds.

That is, first the emotional-physical paradox of dual purposes : the eyes, the inlets of light and vision, are fountains of pain and loss. That leads to the paradox that birth is death, the womb the tomb. And that leads to the social discord which the inner split reflects : the mass of public wrongs.

But on the other side, developing from successful adjustment, is the dialectical sense on the unity of opposites from which emerges a higher unity.

Note the emphasis of the birth-release idea in Birthright as used by Bunyan and his contemporaries. The birthright was that which should have been freely held in common. The individual could come into his own only by sharing in a common heritage. Here *individual* and *common* are the two opposites fusing to produce a more intense notion of human liberty.

The image of an harmoniously organic social life is that of a continuously successful birth, a continuum of perfect adjustment to the changing pressures of environment, of perfect timing between oneself and process.

4. DREAMS

To take some dreams recorded by men living around the same time as Bunyan, and to analyse them briefly to show how the birth-image works in them, will be of value ; for it will adumbrate the method we have used to analyse Bunyan's dream-imagery, and will reveal the common elements of pressure in others of his day.

First, however, let us note that the prominence of the Father and Mother as symbols does not have the sexual significance given it by Freud. The obsession is with the birth-imagery, though of course this imagery is mixed up and fuses with coition-imagery. By laying all the emphasis on sex, Freud shuts the individual up in a closed space of family-relationships. In fact, the desire for contact with the Mother has a deeper and more important basis in *food-needs* ; and since it is through those needs that we first become aware of the world, the desire to repeat the birth-process, to reachieve contact with the Mother in more successful and satisfying forms, is at root an imaging of the desire for social harmony, adjustment to environment.

Here are some dreams that Archbishop Laud set down :

(i) ' I dreamed of the burial of I know not whom and that I stood by the grave. I awaked sad.'

Here we have the birth–death, womb–tomb idea that derives from the sense of hopeless division. Laud is looking for his lost self, the dead child of birth.

We know what political activities took up Laud's waking life. The dream reveals his sense of frustration, his sense of being up against a blank wall through which he cannot penetrate. Hence the birth-image, expressing process, becomes a death-image. Laud sees the funeral of his hopes. He is butting his head against the wall of history.

(ii) ' That night I dreamed of the marriage of I know not whom at Oxford. All that were present were clothed with flourishing green garments. I knew none of them but Thomas Flaxney. Immediately after, without any intermission of sleep that I know of, I saw the Bishop of Worcester, his head and shoulders covered with linen.'

Of course we cannot analyse all the details in these dreams. To do so, we should have to know a vast amount about the most intimate matters of Laud's life. But we can get at the general drift.

In this dream we again have the death-symbol. Marriage equates with birth, coition with emergence from the uterus. Green represents growth, the pricking upstanding leaf, blade, tree. That is the marriage-aspect. Here is everyone full of jollity, merging and developing into new life.

What part Flaxney played in Laud's life we do not know. But one main reason why he comes in here is because of his name Flaxney. Flax is suggested. Flax also sprouts and grows in the sunlight. Thus Flaxney is one of the happy bridal folk, who have wedded with life, who have succeeded in mastering environment. (Laud was a celibate.)

But green is also the colour of decay (*e.g.* ' Where bloody Tybalt, yet but green in earth.'—*Romeo and Juliet*). From flax is made linen, the garb of death. The happy green garments of growth are bleached into the linen of death. Laud sees a Bishop (a self-projection) who is symbolically garbed for death. The birth-image has again become the death-image.

(iii) ' That night I dreamed I went to seek M. St. and found him with his mother sitting in the room. It was a fair chamber. He went away, and I went after but missed him ; and after tired myself extremely ; but neither could I find him nor so much as the house again.'

M. St. was some particular intimate of Laud's. Prynne, Laud's accuser, does not scruple to accuse Laud of homosexual practices with him. Here, however, he is a self-projection of Laud. He is sitting with his mother in a room. He is the fœtus in its sitting position in the womb. It was a fair chamber. Laud wishes he were there. The child gets out of the room-womb. The feeling of birth-trauma is expressed by the endless wanderings all in vain. The lost-self cannot be found. The house (which with its exits and entrances is one of the commonest dream-symbols for the mother-body) is also lost. Laud is homeless in the world, frustrated.

Again we have the birth-image as one of loss.

(iv) ' I dreamed that my mother, long since dead, stood by my bed, and drawing aside the clothes a little, looked pleasantly upon me and that I was glad to see her with so merry an aspect. She then showed to me a certain old man, long since deceased, whom, while alive, I both knew and loved. He seemed to lie upon the ground, merry enough but with a wrinkled countenance. His name was Grove. While I prepared to salute him, I awoke.'

Here we have the Mother and a Father-Substitute. The Mother's act in drawing the clothes aside represents the birth-emergence. (Clothes, enfolding the body, equate with the mother-flesh enfolding the baby.) The old man, the Father, is named Grove. He is one of the green-garbed ones who enjoyed life. (This name gives the reason

NOTES

why Laud chose the old man for the Father-substitute. Grove is the Father as the sprouting green one, a marriage-reveller.) Both the Mother and Father are merry; they are bridal revellers. The posture of lying on the ground suggests both death and coition. The Father and Mother have known what it is to be merry. But Laud, the celibate, is shut out from such merriness.

But it is the failure to achieve contact, to get the social adjustment he desires, which is the driving-force of anxiety.

Here is another dream. This time the dreamer is Dr. Simon Forman, and the date 23 January 1597. I give the dream for some humorous relief. Also because it clarifies what I have said of the last dream of Laud's, and because the image of going through dirty ways is so prominent in *The Pilgrim's Progress.*

' About 3 a.m. I dreamt that I was with the Queen and that she was a little elderly woman in a Coarse white petticoat all unready, and she and I walked up and down the Lanes and closes talking and reasoning of many matters; at Last we came over a thicket close where were many people, and there were two men at hard words, and one of them was a weaver, a tall man with a reddish beard distrait of his wits, and she talked to him, and he spake very merrily with her, and at Last did take her and kisst her. So I took her by the arm and pulled her away and told her the fellow was frantic, and so we went from him, and I led her by the Arm still, and then we went through a dirty lane. And she had a long white smock, very clean and fair, and it trailed in the dirt and her coat behind, and I took her coat and did carry it up a good way, and then it hung too low before. And I told her in talk she should do me a great favour to let me wait on her, and she said I should. . . . And so we talked merrily, and then she began to lean upon me when we were past the dirt, and to be very familiar with me, and methought she began to Love me. And when we were Alone out of sight methought she would have kissed me. And with that I waked.'

The Queen is a Mother-substitute. As in the last dream of Laud's we have the question of lifting or drawing the clothes as a symbol both of birth and coition. In Forman's dream we see that anxiety as to a symmetrical arrangement which is a common form that the sense of discord, failure to achieve harmonious contact, often takes.

The red-headed man is the Father, the red-head having a phallic suggestion. That suggestion is intensified when the man tries to be ' merry ' and embrace the Mother. The child expresses his jealousy. He wants the Mother, the food-source, all his own. He is jealous of the Father's embrace, not because he thinks in sexual terms, but because, thinking in infantile terms, he imagines the embrace as a taking of food from the Mother—food that he covets for himself.

The child, in the dream, succeeds in getting the Mother all for himself. But it is a grown man dreaming, and so the images of birth

259

and food-getting give way to coitional images. The pair get merry and ready for the kiss. Contact is established.

The passage along the dirty lane shows the filth-image of birth. That image results from the identification of the digestive flux with birth-movement as the basic images of process. (The thicket is a genital symbol. See for example furze-bush and Bushy Park in Eric Partridge's *Dictionary of Slang*.)

The date of Forman's dream is early 1597. It was a moment of great political tension. Doleman's *A Conference about the next Succession to the Crown of England* had appeared some fifteen months before ; and the troubles centring round Essex and his ambitions had kept on increasing. When a few months before Forman's dream she passed her ' grand climacteric ' the general fears came to a head ; the Bishop of St. David's had earned a rebuke for offering up a special prayer before her as for one who had reached the stage that saw ' all the powers of the body daily to decay'. Thus, Forman in his mating with the Queen is settling the miseries of his day ; for if Elizabeth had married and had a child, all the anxieties about impending civil-war would never have occurred. That is how people were thinking, and that idea is reflected in Forman's dream. Thus we see that the simple imagery of cornering the Mother for himself and possessing her has been transformed into the wish to reconcile the warring discords of the day. Only a few months previously Shakespeare had been writing :

> England now is left
> To tug and scramble and to part by the teeth
> The unowed interest of proud swelling state.
> Now for the bare-picked bone of Majesty
> Doth dogged war bristle his angry crest,
> And snarleth in the gentle eyes of peace ;
> Now powers from home and discontents at home
> Meet in one line ; and vast confusion waits . . .
> The imminent decay of wrested pomp.

That is the discord Forman reconciles in his dream. Notice that in the early part of the dream there were the two men quarrelling, one of them a weaver. There is an image of the ' discontents at home'. The class-struggle centred round the cloth-trade ; hence the Weaver. ' A weaver was for a long time a synonym for a heretic. . . . Scepticism as to ecclesiastical is closely followed by scepticism as to secular authority.' (Thorold Rogers.) For the use of Weaver as a generic term for Worker, compare : ' England . . . has degenerated. . . . She has not many gentlemen left. We are few. I see nothing to succeed us but a race of weavers.' (Dickens, *Bleak House*.)

NOTES

In short, the personal anxiety, on examination, resolves into a social discord.

Note the *Coarse* white petticoat. Forman himself capitalizes the word. Coarse would also be a contemporary spelling for corpse. Here there is the grave-image that pervades Laud's dreams, the putrefying body in the white shroud. Such an image naturally pairs off with the dirty-lane, the birth-passage as one of filth, corruption. But the fear underlying this kind of distorted imagery, which appears in its strongest form in the images of hell with its heat-blast and stink, always connotes social division and repression. Forman by representing the Queen in her ' corse ' white-smock expresses the fear that she will die and that her death would mean civil war as was generally expected. The weaver appears as the weaver of ' old England's winding-sheet '. The Queen in her shroud, in the dirt, represents the ' imminent decay ' of Shakespeare's lines.

5. THE NATIONAL CHURCH IN THE EARLY NINETEENTH CENTURY

It was the shock of the French Revolution, and Paine's writings, that brought the bourgeois to heel. They rediscovered the value of a State religion. ' It was a wonder to the lower orders, throughout the country, to see the avenues to the churches filled with carriages. This novel appearance prompted the simple country people to inquire, " what was the matter ? " ' (*Annual Register*, 1798.)

But it took more than a generation for the lesson to be fully learned. The response of the populace to the renewed life given to the State-religion was one of violent hostility ; and the impulses of revolutionary Methodism played an important part in fostering and guiding this mood.

' In her servitude to the rich, she (the State-church) had almost overlooked the very existence of the poor. . . .' A perusal of the Bishops' votes in the pages of Hansard's Parliamentary Debates shows that they actually regarded the people with hatred. These bishops were defenders of absolutism, slavery, and the barbarous penal code ; they were the determined enemies of every political or social reform. And the people themselves knew the bishops for their enemies. The then Bishop of Bristol had his palace sacked and burned, the then Bishop of London was prevented from preaching, the Bishop of Lichfield had to run for his life from St. Bride's Church, Fleet Street. Archbishop Howley, entering Canterbury, was mobbed. On November the Fifth effigies of bishops were substituted for that of Guy Fawkes, and the Bishops of Exeter and Winchester were burnt in effigy outside their own palace-gates. The Archbishop of Canterbury's chaplain had a dead cat thrown at him. In 1829 Samuel

Wilberforce wrote to a friend: ' I think that the Church will fall within fifty years'. In 1832 the Rev. Thomas Arnold of Rugby wrote : ' The Church, as it now stands, no human power can save '.

But Wilberforce and Arnold were wrong. They under-estimated the extent to which the bourgeois were rallying to the Church. The mid-Victorian age saw the collaboration of middle class and Church completed, as a barrier against proletarian aggression.

6. CHURCH-FORMATIONS

When I wrote (p. 105) that the dissenting church-formations were efforts to set up ' outside society ' groups of fellowship which showed the desires unrealizable under a class-state, I was arguing from general principles. I have since noticed that there is a remarkable proof of this contention, a direct linking of the dissent-formations and the first gropings for democratic combinations.

After 1815, when there was savage repression of all working-class unions, with great activity among the government agents-provocateur, the reformers, seeking to evade the laws against trade unions and corresponding societies (the first hint of an International), took for their model the Methodist class-system. The ' Political Protestants ' of Hull were the first in the field, 1818. Within a year groups were formed in many towns, such as Leeds, York, Coventry, London.

The Methodist class-system now became the basis of the whole radical movement. Major Cartwright accepted it, and Hunt and Cobbett used it. The Chartist movement was based on it. At the Rochdale Conference of June 1839, the resolution was passed, that ' the country should be formed into districts, and that the system of classes pursued by the Methodists should be adopted by the Chartists in every district '.

Here we have a most remarkable example of the religious formation in transition to a secular formation. The latter aimed at actualizing what remained an emotional aspiration for the religious.

7. ELECTION

Here is the passage referred to on p. 88. It is from *The Case of the Commonalty of the Corporation of Weavers of London truly stated*. It is important to realize how deeply the question of Election in secular forms was stirring the nation; the fight in the Companies for universal suffrage was an important part of it.

' All legal jurisdiction over a number of people or society of men must either be primitive or derivative. Now primitive jurisdiction is undoubtedly in the whole body and not in one or more members, all men being by nature equal to other, and all jurisdictive power over them, being founded by a compact and agreement with them, is invested in one or more persons who represent the whole and by the content of the whole are empowered to govern by such rules of equality towards all as that both governors and governed may know certainly what the one may command and the other must obey, without the performance of which mutual contract all obligations are cancelled and that jurisdictive power returns into its first spring—the people from whom it was conveyed.'

This would be a remarkable passage for the period if written by some isolated thinker. As the expression of the Commonalty of the Weavers it is doubly remarkable. From this fight of the small masters and journeymen in the Companies developed trade-unionism.

SOURCES

ANY writer who deals with the biography of Bunyan must find himself under a heavy debt to Dr. John Brown. My debt is confessed on every page where I deal with the details of Bunyan's life. (*John Bunyan*, by John Brown, revised by F. Mott Harrison.)

For the questions of identifying the landscape of *The Pilgrim's Progress* I have found Charles G. Harper's *The Bunyan Country* most helpful, and I recommend it to anyone wishing to follow the subject farther. Of other studies on Bunyan, that by ' Mark Rutherford ' is the only one I have found of use.

Of the many works by contemporaries of Bunyan that contribute to the picture I draw, the chief are mentioned in the text: Fox's *Journal*, Baxter's *Autobiography*, the Memoirs of Colonel Hutchinson and of Ludlow, the Clarke Papers, the writings of Lilburne and Winstanley, and Walker's *Sufferings of the Clergy*.

Of works on the life of the period, by far the best I know are E. Trotter's *Seventeenth-Century Life in the Country Parish* and M. James's *Social Problems and Policy during the Puritan Revolution*. To this latter book the notes on Enclosures and Utopias owe much.

The Select Works of Crowley, ed. by J. M. Cowper, and Furnivall's *Ballads from Manuscript* are books of the greatest importance on the questions of Enclosure and other social evils. I have not here drawn on the various denouncers of Enclosure in Bunyan's day, chief of whom is the Rev. John Moore, with his magnificent *The Crying Sin of England*.

Matter in the text is drawn from *James Nayler*, by M. R. Brailsford; *Political Ballads*, Wilkins ; *Mutiny*, T. H. Wintringham ; *Life and Times of Martin Blake*, J. F. Chanter ; *History of the Later Puritans*, Marsden ; *Hist. Account*, Calamy ; *History of the Civil War*, Gardiner ; *Herts during the Civil War*, A. Kingston.

The quotation from Sprigge is from *Anglia Rediviva* ; those from Taylor from *The Great Eater of Kent* and *Mad Fashions* ; that on Anabaptists from *A Short History of Anabaptists*, 1642.

The quotation about unemployed psychology in chapter 6 is from *Memoirs of the Unemployed*, 1934 ; ' The Psychology of the Unemployed ' (an appendix), by Morris Robb, M.D. The passage quoted in Note 5 is from *The Freethinker*, 4 April 1937.

Wall's Letter to Milton I quote from Baron's preface to *Eikonoclastes*.

SOURCES

The dreams of Laud are from *Laud* by P. T. Coffin ; that of Forman is to be found in Furnivall's book already mentioned.

For Henslowe (chap. 28) see G. B. Harrison, *Shakespeare at Work.*

The reference to weavers by Thorold Rogers in Note 4 is from his *Industrial & Commercial History of England.*

The passage about the ' dumb dogs ' in the time of the Franciscans is to be found in *Un Nouveau Chapitre* by P. Sabatier.

For the general psychological and anthropological analyses the material can be found in the works of Fraser, Ernest Crawley, &c. It will be clear from the text that while accepting the Freudian technique for finding the physical bases of ideas and symbols, I dissent entirely from Freud's conclusions.

For Black Annis, see *County Folklore*, Leicestershire and Rutland, vol. I. For the *Odyssey* see the writings of V. Berard. *The Timeless Theme*, by Colin Still, is an extremely interesting work on the relation of symbolism and allegory to the elemental world in terms of which man defines his sense of process ; also it finely intuits the social whole from which art arises ; but it ignores the actual forms of social change.

For chapters 5 and 28 there are Miss James's book ; R. H. Tawney, *Religion and the Rise of Capitalism* ; I. Grubb, *Quakerism and Industry before 1800* ; J. A. Hobson, *God and Mammon* ; Chapman Cohen, *Christianity, Slavery and Labour.*

Also of value for the general issues of the period are G. P. Gooch, *English Democratic Ideas in the Seventeenth Century* ; L. Berens, *The Digger Movement* ; W. Curtler, *The Enclosure and Redistribution of Land* ; G. Unwin, *Industrial Organization in 16th & 17th Centuries.*

For the relation of Bunyan to medieval allegory see the well-documented *Life and Pulpit in Medieval England*, by G. R. Owst.

For the material in Note 6, see *Methodism and the Working-Class Movements of England*, by R. F. Wearmouth.

INDEX

INDEX

INDEX